Car Buying and Ownership

John Henderson

For UK order enquiries: please contact Bookpoint Ltd,
130 Milton Park, Abingdon, Oxon OX14 4SB.
Telephone: +44 (0) 1235 827720. Fax: +44 (0) 1235 400454.
Lines are open 09.00–17.00, Monday to Saturday, with a 24-hour
message answering service. Details about our titles and how to
order are available at www.teachyourself.com

For USA order enquiries: please contact McGraw-Hill
Customer Services, PO Box 545, Blacklick, OH 43004-0545, USA.
Telephone: 1-800-722-4726. Fax: 1-614-755-5645.

For Canada order enquiries: please contact McGraw-Hill
Ryerson Ltd, 300 Water St, Whitby, Ontario L1N 9B6, Canada.
Telephone: 905 430 5000. Fax: 905 430 5020.

Long renowned as the authoritative source for self-guided
learning – with more than 50 million copies sold worldwide –
the Teach Yourself series includes over 500 titles in the fields of
languages, crafts, hobbies, business, computing and education.

British Library Cataloguing in Publication Data: a catalogue record
for this title is available from the British Library.

Library of Congress Catalog Card Number: on file.

First published in UK 2007 by Hodder Education, part of Hachette
UK, 338 Euston Road, London NW1 3BH.

First published in US 2007 by The McGraw-Hill Companies, Inc.

This edition published 2010.

Previously published as *Teach Yourself Car Buying and
Maintenance.*

The *Teach Yourself* name is a registered trade mark of
Hodder Headline.

Typeset by MPS Limited, a Macmillan Company.

Printed in Great Britain for Hodder Education, an Hachette UK
Company, 338 Euston Road, London NW1 3BH, by CPI Cox &
Wyman, Reading, Berkshire RG1 8EX.

The publisher has used its best endeavours to ensure that the URLs for
external websites referred to in this book are correct and active at the
time of going to press. However, the publisher and the author have
no responsibility for the websites and can make no guarantee that a
site will remain live or that the content will remain relevant, decent or
appropriate.

Hachette UK's policy is to use papers that are natural, renewable
and recyclable products and made from wood grown in sustainable
forests. The logging and manufacturing processes are expected to
conform to the environmental regulations of the country of origin.

Impression number   10 9 8 7 6 5 4 3 2 1
Year   2014 2013 2012 2011 2010

Contents

Image credits

Front cover: © Tom Hoenig/Getty Images

Back cover: © Jakub Semeniuk/iStockphoto.com, © Royalty-Free/Corbis, © agencyby/iStockphoto.com, © Andy Cook/iStockphoto.com, © Christopher Ewing/iStockphoto.com, © zebicho – Fotolia.com, © Geoffrey Holman/iStockphoto.com, © Photodisc/Getty Images, © James C. Pruitt/iStockphoto.com, © Mohamed Saber – Fotolia.com

Meet the author

A car is usually the second largest purchase we make after a house. But while few would buy a house without professional help, many think nothing of spending thousands on a new car with little more research or care than they would put into replacing their fridge.

I want this book to help the ordinary driver, not the enthusiast or amateur mechanic, to learn responsible car ownership from purchase to trade-in or scrapping. I've tried to make it non-technical and easily understood but to help you, any word in the glossary on page 246 is in bold type when it first appears in the text.

Hopefully, this book will enable you to buy a car as painlessly as possible. Once you have bought the car, this book will help you keep it safe and running efficiently. But no book of this kind is a replacement for your car's handbook. If your handbook says one thing and this book suggests something else, you'd be safer to follow the handbook. This is because it might be a feature that is unique to your car.

Motoring laws and regulations change constantly and vary throughout the world. This book is written for the UK market – your legal responsibilities as a car owner and driver vary greatly around the world, so should be checked locally. While this book will be updated from time to time, you must be aware that legislation changes, so even in the UK there may be differences. If you have any doubt, seek professional advice from a car dealer, government agency or motoring organization.

John Henderson 2010

Only got a minute?

It is not vanity to look after your car, it's common sense.
Taking a financial view, a car is a big investment for anyone,
even if you can only afford an old one, and it makes sense
to protect that investment as much as you can by keeping
it in reasonable condition. But unlike almost any other
purchase, your life can depend on your car and how you
look after it. A neglected washing machine might flood the
kitchen but it is unlikely to kill you. A neglected car may
put you and your family under a truck.

Yet you do not need special skills to keep a car
safe. Anyone can check a tyre's pressure and tread depth,
look at a brake fluid reservoir or read the handbook to see
how often the car needs servicing. Checking oil level on
a dipstick requires no special abilities and nobody needs
instructions on how to clean the windscreen to make it
easier to spot road hazards.

Noticing when things are wrong and doing
something about it can save you money in the long

run because spotting a small fault can stop it becoming a big one.

As you learn about your car, you also become less likely to be taken for a ride. If you know what that uneven tyre wear means you are not going to buy a used car showing it without insisting the seller gets the wheel alignment sorted and replaces the tyres.

Furthermore, if you are more car aware you are much more likely to buy a car that suits your needs and your pocket. You will recognise what is important and what can be ignored when buying a car and are more likely to know the questions to ask. You won't be the sort of person who doesn't think to check whether the boot is big enough or who buys a car with expensive alloy wheels sporting low profile tyres that give a hard ride and are expensive to replace, just because it looks cool.

5 Only got five minutes?

The most important part of buying a car is research, whether you plan to buy a brand new Range Rover or a well-used hatchback. If you find out as much as you can about your choice you are far less likely to make expensive mistakes.

Remember, if you get rid of a car soon after buying it, you lose a lot of money. That is because you lose any taxes paid on it and it is unlikely you will be able to sell it for as much as you paid for it, especially if it was a new car. So, make sure you buy something you can live with.

Whether you are buying new or used, think carefully about your needs. A country dweller with a family and a large dog has very different needs to an urban bachelor. Also check running costs are within your means, including getting insurance quotes – and have a look at depreciation, either by visiting a car pricing website or simply by doing a used car search. All new cars lose more money in the first year than subsequent years (the VAT alone creates a huge 'loss') but some lose more than most, making them an unwise new car buy but a good second-hand prospect.

Look at what equipment the different versions have and decide what is important to you. There is no point paying extra for the top model if a mid-range one has all you want. But if you are buying new and add extras, you will not get that money back when you sell the car, so buying the next model up makes more sense than adding lots of kit. Used car buyers who do not know what was standard on a particular model in a certain year cannot complain if they find it hasn't got air conditioning because it was only standard on the next model up that year.

If you are buying used, try to find out about common faults in the car you want. There are plenty of online sources, or you can have a chat with a friendly mechanic.

Car prices are negotiable. You are unlikely to get a discount on a new model, anything with a waiting list or something rare and desirable, but you might be able to talk them into including accessories or things like extended warranties. New cars dealers often have price leeway to secure sales but, in general, the cheaper the car the less you are likely to get off because the profit margins also shrink.

With used cars, though there are 'book' prices on them, the car is worth what people will pay for it. Many sellers price over the odds with the intention of coming down and if you know this car is priced, say, £1,000 over what the guides say is reasonable, you have a good bargaining start point.

Keep calm when haggling and remember that car sales people are trained negotiators, so don't feel too sorry about pushing the price down – they are not going to sell it for less than they know they can get. If you push them too far down, they'll just dig in and that's when you must decide whether to shake on the deal or walk away. Do not be influenced by claims like 'I've got someone coming to see it this afternoon' if you are not happy with the deal or want to think about it. Call their bluff: if they do sell it, there will be another one; if they don't, you can use it to haggle the price down.

Having gone to all this trouble to get the car you want, look after it. If you have ever bought a second-hand car you know that when you saw one that was obviously not looked after, it created a bad impression and made you less willing to risk buying. If you do not care for your car and keep a service record, you reduce its resale value when you come to sell it. The more your car is worth when you replace it, the less money you must find for the next one.

Looking after it starts with listening to what the sales person tells you on delivery and then reading the handbook when you get home. In the later chapters of this book we explain all the other tricks to keeping it smart, from regular safety checks to cleaning it. Apart from the hard-earned cash this vehicle represents, your safety and convenience also depend on looking after it.

1

Choosing your car

In this chapter you will learn:
- *how to choose a car*
- *how to find finance and insurance*
- *environmental considerations.*

Choosing a car, even if you are not an enthusiast, is a head and heart matter. Your head may say the most sensible car to buy is the economical hatchback but your heart may be won by the small sports car. This is not necessarily a bad thing. Too many people fail to realize that a car is something they have to live with for years, and knowing you have saved lots of money on something sensible or on a showroom bargain soon loses its appeal if you can't stand the sight of the thing on your drive. However, you mustn't let your heart run away with you because the fun will go out of the sports car just as quickly if it doesn't suit your lifestyle or drains your pocket of more than you can afford.

In recent years car designers have excelled at creating cars to meet every need and style. Indeed, the latest evidence is that buyers are moving away from the traditional car classes to seek more style, practicality and individuality. This is one reason why 4×4s have become so popular when so few people actually need their abilities, but it also applies to smaller cars. For example, in Europe there are increasing numbers of what are sometimes called compact **multi-purpose vehicles** (MPVs) which offer the versatility and shape of the large seven-seat MPV 'people carriers' (a 'van' in the USA) but in a five-seat body little bigger than a small hatchback. In many countries, demand for saloons is fading away because of their lack of versatility.

This means however and wherever you live and whatever your budget, within reason, there is something to suit you. However, if you live and work in a large city you should seriously consider whether you really need a car. A car costs you money even when it is parked, through tax, insurance, depreciation and servicing (it still needs to be serviced at least annually), so if it is only being used for the odd shopping trip or the occasional weekend in the country, might you be financially better off taking a taxi or hiring a car for the odd times when public transport is impractical?

Insight

I was shocked to find on a used car website that if I entered a London postcode I found several cars that were three or four years old with less than 5,000 miles on the clock. In fact, one had done less than 1,000 miles a year; just think of the cost per mile the owner was paying!

Size matters

Traditionally, cars are split into classes. Using the Ford European range as examples, because everyone knows what they are, the Ka is class A, Fiesta is B, Focus is C and Mondeo is D, and so on. However, many cars now bridge these classes: compact MPVs often sit between classes B and C while some cars, like Ford Focus C-Max, Volkswagen Golf Plus and Vauxhall's Zafira, are about the same size as a C-class hatch but have the space of a D-class or better. Car classes vary in other markets, as do perceptions. The American and Australian idea of a 'small' car is not the same as the European one. Indeed, the smallest car Ford sells in the USA is the Focus and in Australia it is the Fiesta. But wherever you live, the bigger the car you have, the more money you will spend on fuel, and the more you will be contributing to your world being damaged by people burning more fuel than they need to.

BIGGER ISN'T BETTER

Generally, the bigger the car the more expensive it is to buy and run, though there are exceptions especially among the latest turbodiesels which often give large cars the fuel consumption more usually associated with much smaller ones: you can now get luxury diesel sports saloons which reach 60 **mph** in less than eight seconds but still do better than 50 **mpg**.

These days you do not have to buy a bigger car than you need to get a high level of equipment, safety or refinement. Upmarket versions of even the smallest hatches are now very well equipped and, while bigger and more luxurious cars have extremely high levels of safety and refinement, the gap between them and more mundane cars, in this respect, is shrinking. There are plenty of small hatchbacks in which you cannot hear the engine at motorway speeds, while wind and road noise are also subdued. Manufacturers these days often compete with each other to be able to boast 'best safety in class'.

BIGGER INSIDE

So, your first consideration is to work out how big a car you need. Even if you have a family and need space in the back, don't discount B-class hatches – some have a lot of passenger room for their size. Indeed, many of the latest have more room in the back for long legged people behind a tall driver than some much larger executive saloons. A good indicator of interior space is **wheelbase**, the measurement between the front and rear wheels. The further the wheels are apart, the more room there is to put things between them, so if you have two cars that are the same overall length, the one with the longer wheelbase is likely to have more space. But also consider how this space is used. If you are very tall and have no children, maximum room in the front may be more important to you. If you want a car to carry dogs or scuba gear, a large load area may be more important than rear passenger space.

Think carefully before you go up a size. It might be nice to have the extra space but if you don't need it you are paying for extra metal and, usually, extra fuel to carry it around. However, trying to cram everything into a smaller car than you need is neither convenient nor safe and if you end up having to use a roof rack, fuel consumption will suffer.

> ## Insight
>
> I am tall at 6 ft 2 in and people are often surprised when they see me getting out of a small car saying it's comfortable. But computer-aided design has allowed car designers to make the best of what the industry calls the car's 'packaging', which is the way they fit everything into the space available. Today I often find that even in small cars I can put the driver's seat in my long legged position and am still able to sit comfortably in the seat behind it. True, in a larger car I might be able to spread out more, but the days are gone when all Fiesta-sized cars were only viable transport for two adults and two children. So, before you dismiss the next car size down as 'too small' have a sit in one instead of just looking through the window, and see if it really is as cramped as you expected.

OPENING DOORS

The number of doors is also important and there are two schools of thought here. Some say four doors are always better than two because the car will be easier to sell on and usually retains the extra cost of the back doors. It is also true that even if you do not often carry passengers, the extra doors are more convenient, they often make it easier to lower rear seats and give you extra access to the luggage area when you do.

However, a single person or childless couple may so rarely use the rear doors that, if they are on a tight budget, it is not worth paying several hundred pounds more for a feature they might only need a few times a year. In addition, there are some two door cars where the doors are so long that access to the back is little harder than in a four-door, though even these can be awkward for those with mobility problems. If you have children, remember: getting them strapped into a child seat in the back of a two-door car can be very difficult even with a co-operative child.

Hatchbacks and estate cars are often called three- or five-doors because the hatch is considered to be a door. These are the most versatile of cars, but if load carrying is important, take a good look at that back door, because not all are as practical as they seem. The ideal shape is a hatch that opens as near as possible to the full width of the load area all the way down: there is no point having a wide floor if the lower part of the hatch is only half that width. A hatch that opens as near to the floor as possible also makes loading and unloading much easier.

If you regularly carry large objects, a rear seat that folds completely flat is a must because it makes it easier to slide things in and means objects are totally supported by the floor, not angled up against a sloping seatback.

Engines

Choosing an engine is bound to be a matter of compromise. In general, the more powerful it is, the more fuel it consumes but it is stupid to choose a high economy engine if it can't do what you want. A small, economical engine might haul your chosen car happily through town traffic but if you do a lot of motorway driving it could prove frustrating and a false economy.

BALANCE OF POWER

Do not assume the smallest engine is always the most economical. There is an optimum engine size for the car and the work you intend to do. For example, there is a 1.5 turbodiesel engine used by Nissan and Renault that is available in two power outputs, and the official fuel consumption figures show only slightly better fuel consumption for the more powerful one. But on the road, while both do around 60 mpg in town, taking them onto a motorway sees the lower powered engine's fuel consumption worsen more markedly than the more powerful version's.

In general, a more powerful engine is working less hard when maintaining cruising speeds and accelerating up to speed on faster roads. Similarly, if you want to tow or carry heavy loads, a more powerful engine is likely to manage it better. If you only want to potter around town, however, you'd probably be best opting for the smaller engine, which should still prove more economical.

UNDERSTANDING FIGURES

So how can you tell what engine will suit you best? It helps to understand the engine performance figures quoted in brochures and road test articles. Most people understand 'power', usually expressed as **brake horsepower (bhp)** or **kilowatts (Kw)**, though you may also see it as **PS** which is the abbreviation for the German word for **horsepower**. A kilowatt is 1.341 bhp while 1 PS is 0.986 bhp. This is power like a racehorse going flat out, carrying the car on to its maximum speed.

Car specifications show these figures as 'X bhp or **lb ft** at Y,000 **rpm**'. This means the engine develops its maximum power, or **torque** (represented by 'lb ft' – see below), at that many engine revolutions (**revs**) per minute (rpm). This can give you important clues as to how that engine feels. Generally, if the engine revs shown are high, it needs to be worked hard to get the best from it.

TORQUE EXPLAINED

The less understood torque is more important than horsepower for day-to-day driving. Torque is often described as the twisting power of the engine – what gets the wheels turning. Think of it like the energy you see as a heavy horse leans into the collar and starts a cart moving. Many people call it pulling power and it is what gives the car its gutsy flexibility. Flexibility means having to work it less hard, having to change gear less and getting more relaxed cruising where the car maintains and regains speed more easily. Torque is usually shown as **pounds-feet (lb ft)** or the metric **Newton Metres (Nm)**. A Newton Metre is 0.738 lb ft.

With torque, the lower the engine revs the better as this means the engine will show good flexibility from low speeds. However, a good spread of torque is also important, meaning that the engine develops useful levels of it across a wide rev range. Some diesels hold their torque peak for a long time, so the specification might read '200 lb ft 1,800–2,550 rpm' which suggests extreme flexibility. With the right **gearbox** you might be able to keep it in or near that 750 rpm range from 60–70 mph in top gear giving you very relaxed, flexible and economical cruising and good progress on country roads in higher gears.

Sometimes you see engine performance expressed as a simple graph with a steep curve for power and a flatter one for torque (see Figure 1.1). They usually show engine revs across the bottom with power up one side and torque up the other. This can tell you a lot

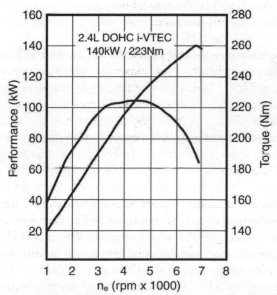

Figure 1.1 This torque graph for a Honda 2.4 litre petrol engine shows that while torque (flatter curve) peaks at fairly high revs, flexibility is assured by good output at lower revs.

more than the bare figures by showing you how the engine delivers its performance. For example, you might have a petrol engine which develops peak torque at fairly high revs, but the graph shows how it produces more than, say, 85 per cent of that peak over 2,000 or 3,000 rpm and would be much more flexible than the bare figures suggest.

This may sound very technical, but it is worth understanding because it will stop you discounting cars for the wrong reason (and mean nobody can baffle you with 'torque talk'). For example, many people look at 0–60 mph or 0–62 mph (100 kph) standing start figures as the ultimate indicator of acceleration and are then baffled that a car that takes longer to hit 60 mph feels so much quicker on the road, as is often true with diesels. That is because a car with a good torque spread but lower power is likely to be much more flexible in normal driving than one with a lesser torque spread and higher power, which shows if top gear 50–70 mph acceleration is quoted. Unless you are a bit of a boy racer, you are unlikely to want to send a car wheel spinning from standstill to hit 60 mph as quickly as possible, but you often want to accelerate from 50 to 70 in top gear.

So, those are the characteristics you are looking for. The next choice is petrol or diesel.

DIESEL

Diesel sales are booming all over Europe, with good reason. Though these engines are almost always more expensive to buy than petrol engines, because they are more expensive to produce, fuel economy is between 20 and 30 per cent better than equivalent petrol units. This used to mean suffering a lot of extra noise and sluggish performance but that is no longer the case and the latest generation diesels give little clue to the fact that there is anything different under the bonnet – if anything, it will usually only be that they have a deeper sound.

Many dealers will sit you down and do calculations based on your mileage to point out that you will never get the difference in cost back on fuel savings. However, you will get a substantial lump of it back, good diesels currently hold their value well and the best of them are so much nicer to drive than petrol engines of similar, or even inferior, economy that these facts alone can make them worth more. This is particularly true of smaller cars where the diesels have a much more drivable nature than small petrol engines can manage. Indeed, on car press launches it is increasingly common for the after drive talk among journalists to be how the diesel is the best of the bunch. There are even hot hatch, convertible and roadster diesels now, offering style and sporty performance with high economy.

If you need or want a 4×4, a diesel is really the only sensible option, bringing fuel consumption into affordable realms and significantly improving its resale values (if a buyer can afford petrol off-roader consumption, they can afford to buy a new one). Diesels also have the ideal power delivery for the towing and off-road work these vehicles do in rural areas.

PETROL

Despite the view of diesel cars above, if you do very low mileage in an ordinary car it can be difficult to justify the extra cost of a diesel and most car models come with a much wider range of petrol engines. Increasingly, the larger petrol engines are designed for flexibility rather than power while modern fuel systems, like direct petrol injection, drastically improve fuel efficiency.

HYBRID

A few cars are powered by petrol electric **hybrid** systems, with the first diesel electric hybrid launched in 2010. Here the conventional engine is supplemented by an electric motor with a battery pack. The fuelled engine charges the batteries and cuts in when the power demanded is more than the electric motor can deliver. Petrol hybrids are popular in America and Japan (where diesels are unpopular for historical reasons) and with Westminster politicians because they can look green while avoiding London congestion charging, but it is debatable whether their exemption from the charge is justifiable. The theory is that at low speeds they run on non-polluting electric power but in practice they can only do this at very low speeds and when fully charged, so much of the time they run on petrol or a combination of petrol and electric. True, the petrol engine cuts out when the car halts in traffic jams and restarts automatically, but there are conventional engined cars that do the same, and there is nothing to stop you turning the key.

Cost has been their biggest drawback with the difference between petrol and petrol electric as much as five times the difference between petrol and diesel. However, cheaper models are appearing that cost little more than rival diesels. But for all the extra technology, the fuel economy of a petrol hybrid is not much better than a diesel's, while there are also concerns about the high-energy use during manufacture and recycling batteries.

There is more information on greener fuel options in the section on environmental concerns later in this chapter.

Insight

The official EU fuel consumption figures are unusually kind to hybrid cars because the test's urban cycle is so gentle that they run on electric power much more than in real-life traffic. The British magazine *What Car?* found when comparing EU consumption figures with more realistic tests that all EU figures are optimistic but the greatest difference between official and test consumption figures was in hybrid cars. As a rural driver, I achieve nothing like the official figures when testing hybrid cars, yet with diesels may even do better.

FUEL PROS AND CONS

Diesel pros	Diesel cons
Good economy	Dearer to buy
Lower emissions	A few are loud
Safer than petrol	Fuel smell lingers on hands and clothes

Diesel pros	Diesel cons
Good driving flexibility	Older diesels' emissions not as clean as petrol
Good ones hold their value well	Disliked in America for historical reasons
Considerable tax advantage on fuel in some countries	
Greater range from a tank full	
Most diesel is at least partly plant derived	
Some small diesels avoid congestion charges	

Petrol pros	Petrol cons
Cheaper cars to buy	Higher CO_2 emissions
Wide range of engines	Its vapour ignites easily and explosively
Fuel soon evaporates if spilled	Less range than diesel from the same sized tank
Higher powered engines	Solely a fossil fuel

Hybrid pros	Hybrid cons
Lower emissions than equivalent petrol engines	Expensive to buy
Good flexibility as electric and petrol work together	Higher energy use in manufacture than conventional engines
Shuts petrol engine off in jams	Rarely runs on electric alone

(Contd)

Hybrid pros	Hybrid cons
Zero emissions when running on electric	Complex
Avoids congestion charging	Batteries have limited life and must be carefully recycled
Tax concessions in some countries	Heavier than equivalent petrol cars
	Diesels usually match their economy and emissions
	Same safety drawbacks as petrol cars

Gearboxes

Choosing between a manual or automatic gearbox is largely a matter of personal preference. Modern automatics often perform well, responding quickly and rarely getting in the way of spirited driving. A few even offer the same performance and economy as manual gearboxes.

Basically, the more gears you have available, the better. All new cars have at least a five-speed manual box, though, increasingly, high performance models and the better diesels have six speed.

Diesels' high torque means they can often cope with very tall top gears for extremely relaxed cruising. Some high performance cars though, have a sixth gear no taller than most ordinary cars' fifth, but this allows the ratios between the other gears to be 'closer'. This means when you change gears up or down, the change in engine speed is not so great, making it easier to keep the engine in its most responsive rev range.

AUTOMATICS

Most automatics are four- or five-speed, though six-speed automatics are becoming more common and some luxury cars have seven- or even eight-speed gearboxes. Modern automatics also often offer a choice of 'normal' or 'sports' modes, where the latter holds gears longer, responds more quickly to use of the throttle and, in some, avoids using top gear. Increasingly they have a manual touch-change, sometimes called a **sequential shift**, pioneered by Porsche with its **Tiptronic** system. This allows you to shift up and down in sequence manually by tapping the lever back and forth or using steering wheel mounted paddles and can be used when extra control or quicker responses for harder driving are required.

True automatics have a device called a **torque converter**, which uses hydraulics to move between gears as required, but there are an increasing number of automatic and semi-automatic gearboxes with some sort of electronic **clutch**. Some are very good, like Volkswagen's Dynamic Shift Gearbox, which uses two clutches so one is getting the next gear ready while the other is engaged, but some of those in smaller cars produce very jerky shifts in auto mode, especially at modest speeds, so check you can live with them in town.

CVT

You may also come across continuously variable gearboxes or **continuously variable transmissions (CVT)**. This is an automatic box but, instead of having a combination of set gears to engage, it has electronically controlled pulleys and steel belts which, as the name suggests, continuously vary the ratio being used. That means they ideally match themselves to the demands being made on the engine. Early ones in the 1980s were strange beasts but modern ones work well, often allowing small engines to cruise at amazingly low revs. They shift more smoothly than some of the other small car automatics and require a slightly different driving style: for example, if you want them to shift up when you reach cruising speed you often have to ease off the throttle.

A good automatic is a boon in town driving, reducing stress on the driver, which is why some of the semi-automatics can be so disappointing here. It is much harder to abuse an automatic and virtually impossible to stall one. Hill starts are also easier, though most drivers feel a manual gives better overall control. Manuals also tend to be cheaper to buy and most of them still have better fuel consumption, though the differences are getting smaller all the time.

Insight

When I started out in motoring journalism in the early 1980s I would never have bought an automatic. Most seriously blunted a car's performance, they came nowhere near the control a manual gave and they seriously hit fuel economy. Small car automatics were just starting to come out and some of these were truly awful, often being totally unresponsive. But electronics helped transform the auto gearbox. Modern **engine management** and gearbox electronics are integrated to work together so, for example, when shifting, the engine management adjusts the throttle, regardless of what the driver is doing, to give a smooth change. The result is that modern automatics usually drive well and are often as responsive as a well-driven manual. They have much less impact on fuel economy and some, like VW's DSG box mentioned above, can even be more economical than a manual. I now own an automatic and urge anyone who previously dismissed them to take another look.

GEARBOX PROS AND CONS

Manual pros	Manual cons
Cheaper to buy	Harder work for the driver especially in town
Fuel economy is usually better	Requires more skill from the driver to change smoothly
Mechanically more simple	Clumsy drivers can stall the car

Automatic pros	Automatic cons
Easy relaxed driving	Fuel consumption is higher on all but the most modern
Virtually impossible to stall one	Only the best offer drivers as much control as a manual
Difficult to abuse one	Mechanically more complex
Hill starting easier	With most, performance is poorer than with a manual

Environmental concerns

We should all take steps to reduce our lifestyle's impact on the environment, and the motor industry has done more than most to help us achieve this.

Top tip

As a rule of green thumb, the newer a car's design, the cleaner it is likely to be. You do not help the environment by buying an old car because manufacture is a tiny proportion of the car's whole-life emissions and modern cars are also cleaner in that respect.

The above even applies to modern cars with higher fuel consumption than older ones. Global warming fears mean many now tend to think no further than carbon dioxide (CO_2) output and forget that car exhausts can include far worse pollutants. This is especially so of petrol cars so old they do not have **catalytic converters**: get shut in a garage with one of those and the carbon monoxide renders you unconscious long before the smell of the unburned hydrocarbons and oxides of sulphur and nitrogen become offensive and you die shortly after that. Catalytic converters in the exhaust break these gases down into harmless, or less harmful, ones while modern fuel injection and engine management systems ensure the engine runs at optimum efficiency, even matching the amount of fuel injected to the amount of oxygen in the air as altitude and temperature increase.

Since the pre-catalyst days, legislators around the world have set ever-higher standards for emissions. California and Japan were ahead of everyone else but Europe has set a succession of increasingly cleaner standards. Euro One came in in July 1992 and stricter standards have been introduced roughly every four years since then with **Euro5** required from September 2009 and Euro Six set to arrive in September 2014. Engines to the current standard are the cleanest ever made.

Generally, the lower a car's fuel consumption, the less it pollutes. Older diesels do create more **particulates** and oxides of nitrogen and sulphur than petrol engines but most experts say that, overall, they still pollute less than petrols. Indeed, from Euro5 on, diesels must have the same particulate output as petrols. Successive UK governments have claimed this is not so (to justify extra road tax on diesels) but they are the only European government that takes this view.

FUEL FROM PLANTS

Biofuels are now coming into play and if the UK government gives in to pressure from the fuel and motor industries to follow other countries and give more tax incentives on their production, sale and use, it could take off. Biofuels are made from vegetable matter, which means they are renewable sources. But in addition, when you burn them you only release back into the atmosphere the CO_2 absorbed by the plants as they grew. With fossil fuels you are releasing CO_2 that has been laid down and trapped over millions of years.

BIODIESEL

Most diesel fuel sold in the UK now has some **biodiesel** in it. This is diesel made from various types of new and used vegetable oil and though pure biodiesel is sold in some countries, not all diesel engines can run on it. All diesels will run on mixtures that are about 5 per cent biodiesel, which does seem to smooth their running and slightly improve consumption, as well as cleaning emissions. A few modern diesels can run on mixes as high as 30 per cent biodiesel, but at the moment you'd need to buy in bulk from a limited number of suppliers to get it.

BIOETHANOL

Bioethanol is an alcohol made from sugar beet, which is widely grown in the UK, as well as grain, sugar cane and wood chippings. The fuel must be 15 per cent petrol to aid starting, but is otherwise plant derived. You need a specially adapted engine, and in the UK there has not been a great expansion of the number of filling stations selling the fuel so it is mostly only available in East Anglia and the West Country. Fortunately, the engines also run on petrol, or any mixture of petrol and bioethanol, which is why most car companies call their bioethanol models something implying they run on more than one fuel, like Ford's '**Flexifuel**'.

Insight

I am wary of presenting biofuels as the great green cure-all. Though several governments, including the UK's, want to increase the use of biofuels, the jury is still out on how environmentally friendly this is. Several environmental and conservation bodies have objected because of the impact huge monocultures have on wildlife and the way some countries are clearing species-rich rainforest to plant oil palms for biodiesel. Human welfare bodies also object for two main reasons. Firstly, where fuel crops are more profitable than food crops it reduces food production, and secondly, in some countries the use of food crops to make bioethanol has increased the price of staple foods. For example, the Mexican poor, for whom cornflour is an important foodstuff, have been hit by increases in the price of maize due to US bioethanol production demands. Some people say this problem will disappear with new production methods where any part of the plant can be used to make bioethanol, so the food part of the plant can go untouched. However, plant 'waste', like straw, is often used for farm animal feed and bedding. So, if you are environmentally concerned, do not leap at a biofuel car until conservation and welfare organizations give them the green light.

ELECTRIC

Electric cars are becoming more widely available but their limited range is still a problem outside cities. Even as the range is improved, recharging times may still hit their practicality. After all, when you near the end of a conventionally fuelled car's range you can fill it in minutes enabling hundreds of miles more driving, yet, unless we see a battery breakthrough, electric cars take hours to recharge.

In addition, electric cars may produce zero pollution locally but they are still not pollution-free because they are recharged using electricity generated largely by burning fossil fuels. Of course, you can get round that by recharging it using your own renewable power source, if you are prepared to make the investment.

Electric cars using **fuel cells**, which generate electricity by ion transfer, are in the experimental stages. They unite hydrogen fuel with oxygen from the air so the only exhaust gas is water vapour.

RECYCLING

Modern cars are around 85 per cent recyclable and almost every piece of plastic in a car has recycling information on it, so if you change a component or decide a car must be scrapped, make sure you dispose of it in a way that ensures it is recycled. See the end of Chapter 12 for more information.

Safety

The car industry is well ahead of most car buyers on safety issues. Sadly, though it is no longer only the Swedish car-makers pushing safety, the old adage that 'safety doesn't sell' still seems to be true. Too many people think 'it won't happen to me' and those who actively seek cars with high safety ratings and maximum **airbags** tend to be those who have found out the hard way that these things are worth having. But safety is not a waste of money and is an important car-buying consideration that could save your life. People often underestimate the forces involved in an accident and the speed at which things happen. The braking distance at 30 mph is 14 metres, and that would throw you forwards hard, but in a crash the car stops in the length of its own bonnet (you hope) so even at only 30 mph you're thrown forward with a force equivalent to 30 times your own weight.

SEATBELTS

Fitting seatbelts in cars has been mandatory for many years so you are unlikely to buy anything, other than a classic, without them. **Inertia-reel seatbelts** allow freedom of movement and lock if pulled suddenly. Most cars on the road today have these in the front and the two outer rear seats. Some cars may have a fixed lap belt only in the middle rear seat but many modern cars replace this with a three-point inertia-reel belt which is far safer (see Plate 1).

Seatbelt pre-tensioners add to the belts' effectiveness. When an impact occurs they react in fractions of a second to tighten the belt, removing any slack and compressing padded clothes to catch you that bit quicker. Most cars have these on the front seats now and some luxury cars also have them in the back.

HEAD RESTRAINTS

Head restraints are not head rests, but an important safety feature, working with seatbelts and saving you from a potentially crippling injury. In a crash, when you go back into the seat after the belt has caught you, or if the car is hit from behind, your neck is whipped back with great force. At best you get neck ache for a few days, but at worst it can cause you to become a paraplegic or even prove fatal. A properly adjusted head restraint can stop this happening, so check your chosen car has ones that can be adjusted so the top is at least at your eye level. Sadly, some cheap cars still do not have head restraints in the back.

AIRBAGS

However effective seatbelts are, your body still folds forwards on impact, which brings the driver's head and chest down on the wheel while the passengers' heads either hit the fascia or the backs of the front seats. In addition, limbs are thrown around, glass may come flying out of the side windows and, in side-impacts and roll-overs, your head can be smashed sideways and doors can be crushed against occupants. This is where airbags come in.

These are devices hidden behind the car's interior trim which, when triggered by an impact, inflate to cushion and protect. Most systems require at least two sensors to be satisfied there is an impact so the likelihood of them being triggered unnecessarily is low. When they do go off it is with a pop that you're unlikely to notice in a crash. A full-size driver's airbag is fully inflated in about half the time it takes to blink so they do their job so quickly most people are unaware they've gone off until they see the collapsed bag after the crash. They deflate instantly, so will not get in your way if you still need to steer the car.

In short, you have nothing to fear from airbags – unless you plan to try taking the steering wheel or fascia apart – and the more of them you have, the safer you will be.

Most new cars now have at least a driver's airbag in the steering wheel and a front passenger airbag in the fascia above the glovebox. If you need to put a child seat on the front passenger seat, make sure the passenger airbag can be disabled.

Other airbags a car may have are side, curtain and knee bags (see diagram on page 93). Side bags protect against side impacts and are placed in the sides of the seats, usually only the front ones. Curtain airbags drop down over the side windows to protect occupants' heads from hitting the glass or pillars and some are full length while others only protect the front passengers. Knee airbags are still fairly rare and are located in the steering column to protect the driver's knees. A few luxury cars also have airbags in the backs of the front seats to protect back seat passengers.

If any of these bags are extras in a new car it is worth buying them if you can afford them, but be aware that when you trade a car in you rarely get back the cost of extra safety items.

CHILD SAFETY

If you have young children, cars with **Isofix** child seat fixings are worth seeking. This is an International Standards Organization system for fitting child seats that locks the seat to the car's body (the seat has to be Isofix, too). This is much safer because the seat effectively becomes part of the car and the system is intended to be foolproof after it was found that around 80 per cent of non-Isofix seats were incorrectly fitted. (See Chapter 4 for child seat recommendations.)

NCAP

All cars have to comply with international safety legislation relating to how they cope with a crash, but newer cars are generally safer. Look out for details of how the car fared in the **New Car Assessment Programme** (**NCAP**), of which there are European and American versions. This is an independent test programme where cars are crash tested and rated for adult and child occupant safety as well as pedestrian impact safety.

Goodies

Some luxury and convenience equipment is well worth having, while other gadgets are not worth the bother. We'll talk about the effect equipment has on the car's value at trade-in in other chapters but it is worth explaining what a few do and how worthwhile they are.

MORE THAN COOL

Air conditioning (air con) isn't just a summer luxury. It helps clean the air coming into the car, which is a boon for allergy sufferers and means they don't have to drive with the windows open at the height of the hayfever season or in heavy traffic fumes. Modern systems also use less fuel than the drag created by driving with the windows open and in the winter it speeds demisting. It is well worth paying extra for.

HOT SEAT

Heated seats and mirrors may sound trivial but have serious benefits. Heated seats reduce the risk of back pain: think how you tense your muscles when you sit on a cold seat. With leather seats they are an essential worth paying for because, although leather is luxurious, it does get very cold. Heated mirrors not only clear frost from awkward-to-get-at glass but enable you to clear them of mist and spray to preserve your view behind. View them as a safety item worth having, as is electric mirror adjustment for its ease of use on the move.

Electric seat adjusters offer very fine adjustment of seating positions with safe adjustment on the move. For families, seats with a memory facility mean everyone can have their ideal position memorized. The convenience and fine adjustment they allow makes them worth a little extra. (See Plate 2.)

FROST FREE

Heated front screens are of more limited use. In most cars the ventilation system, especially with air conditioning, is more than capable of demisting, though if you live where heavy frosts are common it may be worth having a heated screen for the coldest winter days because it is more effective than defrosting spray. However, they create haloes round oncoming car's headlights which can be distracting. They are worth having if standard, but not worth paying extra for.

SUNROOF

The UK was unique in its love for sunroofs, but even here their popularity has slumped. If the car does not have air conditioning a sunroof is worth having – tilting the sunroof open increases the airflow through the vents without increasing drafts. But sunroofs increase wind noise, even when closed, create another possible source of rattles and leaks and reduce headroom. If the choice is between sunroof and air conditioning, go for the latter.

Insight

If you are tall do not order a sunroof on a car unless you can sit in the same model with one fitted. Most sunroofs steal headroom and for tall people can turn a comfortable car into one you can't possibly live with. Beware of the car in which the sunroof frame just touches the side of your head but you have enough room under the glass: you may find it acceptable in the showroom but out on the road you will be constantly banging your head on the frame. Eventually you start sitting with your head tilted to one side which becomes, literally, a pain in the neck.

HIGH TECH

Bluetooth handsfree is not worth paying extra for unless the dealer can show you that it provides useful functions with your phone. Some systems do not allow access to the phone's address book and there are even some that do not allow you to transfer the address book data from phone to car, making them pretty useless. Most in-car systems are dearer than portable ones which sometimes work better.

The same can now be said of **satellite navigation**. In-car **sat navs** often tie in with the car's other systems, giving easier control of trip computers and air conditioning, but you pay many times more than you would for a portable sat nav that works as well, if not better, and can be used in other cars or on foot. However, with a portable system you must find a place to put it where you can see and reach it but where it will not obstruct airbags, which may be difficult in some cars. Also, portable ones are tempting for thieves if they and their mounting brackets are not hidden or removed when parked.

Voice recognition gives the ability to control things, like the stereo, by voice, but it never lives up to the promise. The handbooks often have pages of phrases you have to remember and the slightest background noise, even from a coarse road surface, stops them understanding your order. Most frustrating of all, when you swear at them they primly say 'I did not understand that'.

HI-FI

Most cars are now supplied with reasonable audio systems and if you choose to upgrade it is money you can't expect to get back on trade-in. Before you upgrade make sure you check what it has. People often see a car which appears to only have a radio and don't realize it has a hidden CD autochanger, which stores several CDs and allows you to choose from a playlist or by pressing a numbered button. Autochangers are worth having for the convenience and because it stops you fumbling with CDs on the move.

If you download music there are two options. Some CD players can play MP3 files from a CD or memory stick and many manufacturers now offer MP3 player (iPod) connection to the car's audio as standard or an option. Increasingly, car and audio manufacturers are including USB sockets which not only offer an alternative way of connecting MP3 players but allow you to play music from cheap memory sticks or to recharge your mobile phone.

Top tip

Always go for audio with large, clearly labelled buttons for easy use on the move. Having main controls duplicated on the steering wheel or a steering column pod is worth extra for safety alone.

Additional costs

Buying a car is not the end of the costs you have to bear so check you can afford it. You must consider:

- ▶ *depreciation*
- ▶ *servicing*
- ▶ *tax*
- ▶ *insurance.*

DEPRECIATION

Depreciation is the biggest cost after fuel. All cars, except some extremely rare and sought after ones, depreciate. The worst depreciation is in the first year, partly because as soon as it leaves the showroom you lose several thousand pounds worth of VAT. From there on depreciation varies a lot from model to model according to its desirability, reputation and supply (if there are a lot of them around they lose money faster).

Some car magazines' specification pages include an estimate of how much a car will be worth in three years but there are also car price guides you can look at and some car-selling websites include depreciation information. These will give you an idea of how a car holds its value but take care with a new model because it may do better than a previous, not so well designed version.

SERVICING

Servicing is easier to check. Generally, a car with a long service interval costs less because it needs less attention, though this may be academic if you do low mileage because manufacturers normally say servicing is required every so many thousand miles or every year. So, if you only do 8,000 miles a year you'll need to get it serviced annually even if the interval is 10,000 or 18,000 miles between services. However, some older cars need an intermediate service, say, every 6,000 miles or six months. This is usually little more than an oil change, but it adds costs. A dealer should be able to give you a ballpark figure for a service, but when you compare them make sure you are comparing like with like because though a car may be serviced every 10,000 miles, more may need to be done at 20,000 and 30,000.

TAX

Every country has some form of road tax, properly called Vehicle Excise Duty in the UK. On vehicles registered since 2003 VED is based on carbon dioxide output, quoted as CO_2 grammes per kilometre (**g/Km**). Cars first registered before that date are taxed based on engine size, which means you can pay less tax for running an old car that pollutes more.

INSURANCE

Insurance can be very frustrating to buy because there are so many variables. In general, the newer, more expensive and more powerful the car and the younger the driver, the more you pay. But where you live, what you do for a living, whether you are married and what sex you are all have an effect on premiums. If you already have insurance, get a quote for the car you are planning to buy to see how much more or less it will cost than your current one. That gives you an idea of whether it is affordable, but seek quotes from other companies when you do buy the car because you may get better deals elsewhere.

Do not assume that because the car is the same insurance group as your current one it will cost the same, the fact that it is newer has a bearing on how much you pay.

Top tip
If this is your first car, get a couple of quotes to help decide if it is affordable before you choose the car. Most insurers won't mind if you explain what you are doing and ask for quotes for two or three different models.

There are two main types of insurance: comprehensive and third party, fire and theft. The former covers everything so if your car is damaged the insurance company pays for the repairs to it even if nobody else was involved: this is the cover to have if the car is a decent one. Third party, fire and theft only covers what the name suggests – if you have an accident the insurance company pays for repairs to the other person's car, but not yours so it is only cost effective if the car is a cheap one you can afford to write-off if repairs are expensive. Whatever insurance you buy, read the policy so you know what you are covered for and check that the paper work shows the correct details for you and your car.

Insight

I recently spoke to a man who had not checked his new insurance paperwork until after he had been stopped by the police who said the computer showed no insurance for his car. It turned out his certificate showed one wrong letter in the car's registration. Foolishly, he also failed to seek legal advice and pleaded guilty by post to driving without insurance. Apart from the mitigating circumstances, he had fully comprehensive insurance that gave him the legal minimum cover on any other car so it is unlikely he had committed an offence. Failing to check the paperwork cost him dear.

BROKER OR DIRECT?

Brokers

The simple way of getting insurance is to use a broker who should get the best quote from a number of insurance companies. However, the fact that you can get different quotes from different brokers shows they are not always as thorough as they claim. You may also find brokers do not give the best quotes if you are young, have a poor driving record, if you want to insure something unusual or if you have an unusual job or one they consider high risk (anything from pop star to a professional like a doctor or journalist). If you are a young pop star with licence points wanting to insure a Ferrari, this is probably not the best way. The many online instant quote websites often become far from instant in these circumstances, usually asking you to ring them after filling in many pages of questions.

Insight

If you use an online comparison site, which is basically an electronic broker, make sure you also get a quote direct from the insurers the site says are cheapest. Car magazines running checks on this have seen people make considerable savings by seeking a direct quote instead of accepting the comparison site's figure. When I tried it one direct quote was £20 cheaper than that given on the comparison site.

Direct

If there is anything unusual about you or the car, you are often better off seeking quotes direct from insurers. If you have a specialist car, check adverts in magazines for that marque or type or join an owners' club to look for favourable rates. If the problem is your job, look in your trade magazines for adverts from insurers. New drivers taking the Pass Plus course (ask your driving instructor) can get discounts, as can members of advanced driving organizations. Some car manufacturers have set up insurance schemes for their cars which can provide cheaper quotes especially for unusual marques, though, again, your individual circumstances can erode the preferential rates.

Broker pros	Broker cons
Simple way of doing it	You still have to phone more than one for the best quote
They should get quotes from several insurers	They can't always cope with 'unusual' cars or drivers
Sometimes offer extras	They add an extra tier between you and the insurer when trying to sort out difficulties
	They don't always check other insurers at renewal time

Direct pros	Direct cons
You know who you're insured with	Not all insurers will deal direct
You deal direct with them over all issues	It's up to you to get other insurers' quotes at renewal
It's easier to get quotes for 'unusual' cars and drivers	
Often cheaper than brokers who are supposed to have tried everyone	

MAKING COMPARISONS

When comparing quotes, make sure you compare like with like. A policy that gives you a loan car in the event of an accident, does not require a big excess or includes additional cover on certain items, may be worth paying more for. Glass cover that does not affect no claims bonuses is also worth having, especially when a stone thrown up by another car can mean replacing a windscreen costing several hundred pounds. If you have accrued a no claims bonus, especially a long one, make sure the policy includes protection for it which means you won't lose a big reduction in annual premiums for making one claim.

CUTTING COSTS

There are many, sometimes surprising ways to keep premiums down:

1 *Volunteer to pay a higher 'excess', which is the first few hundred pounds of a claim. You may be able to claim this back from another driver's insurance if you were not to blame.*
2 *Limit the drivers to named people.*
3 *If you do unusually low mileage you may be able to get a discount but check what happens if you go over the mileage limit set by the premium. You don't want to be worrying if, say, you have to make frequent long journeys to see a sick relative.*

4 *Have a relationship: young men putting a woman on the policy as a second named driver can sometimes get a reduction because it suggests the stabilizing influence of a long-term relationship. Likewise, married couples usually pay less than singles in similar circumstances. There may eventually be an insurance company that does the same for gay couples who have entered civil partnerships.*

5 *Be a woman: some companies offer discounts for cars driven only or mainly by women because, as a group, they have fewer and less serious accidents.*

6 *Get a driving qualification: new drivers taking the UK's Pass Plus additional tuition course can get discounts, as can those who pass advanced driving tests like those run by the Institute of Advanced Motorists and the Royal Society for the Prevention of Accidents.*

GAP INSURANCE

If you are buying a new or nearly new car seek Guaranteed Asset Protection (GAP) insurance. Cars are insured for their market value but a new car's depreciation is high in the first year, so there may be a substantial difference between market value and what you owe on finance or what it would cost to replace it. GAP insurance promises to pay the full replacement cost during the first year or 18 months. It is included in some comprehensive insurance policies and can be bought as part of some finance packages, though it is usually cheaper online.

TELL THE TRUTH

Whatever you do, don't lie to the insurers about yourself or the car. These days they have many databases on which to check information and you may also have forgotten what you said by the time you have an accident. Lying is classed as fraud and can render your insurance void. Parents should not be tempted to insure a child's car putting one of the parents as the main driver, especially for a student living away from home. This, again, is defrauding the insurers and it means the young person is not building up their own no-claims bonus.

Breakdown cover

Breakdown cover is really another form of insurance – you insure against having a breakdown. The best-known organizations are the AA and RAC but there are others like Green Flag and Britannia. Some insurers offer breakdown cover as an addition to your policy using specialist firms such as Mondial Assistance. The best thing is to visit their websites or get their pamphlets and see which organization offers the cover that best suits your needs. If you have special needs, carefully check what exclusions there are. For example, they all say they recover trailers if the towcar can't be fixed, but in the exclusions they may reveal that they will not recover trailers with livestock on board – little use if you tow a horse trailer.

Most do a basic roadside assistance service where they come and try to fix the car at the side of the road and charge extra if it can't be fixed there and needs recovery. They then add various recovery services ranging from simple 'get-you-home' to ones where they put you up in a hotel for the night if they can't. Home call-outs mean they will get the car started if it breaks down at home, while European cover extends the service to the whole of Europe if you frequently go abroad.

But before you rush to join up, check you're not duplicating something you get for free. All new car warranties and manufacturer-approved used car warranties include some breakdown cover, though unlike private membership, they only cover that car. Some new car warranties only give breakdown cover for the first year of a three-year warranty and a few only guarantee to get the car to the nearest dealer, not to get you home from the motorway at 2 a.m. on a Sunday morning. If you are already a member of a breakdown service and buy a car where it is included in the warranty, most organizations allow you to postpone the membership for the period of the warranty cover.

Breakdown cover is always worthwhile, especially if you have limited car knowledge or are likely to be vulnerable if you break down (all breakdown services give priority to lone women, people with children and the disabled). Even if the car is new, silly things happen like losing your keys or finding you left the lights on all day. Indeed, flat batteries are the commonest call out. The risk of breakdown increases with the age of the car so the more vital backup becomes. In addition, calling out a garage is likely to cost a lot more than membership, especially more than the basic membership fees. Many people do not realize that if you break down on a motorway and are not off the hard shoulder in two hours, the police are empowered to call their duty garage to remove your car, which the garage can hold until you have paid their fees. Those fees are usually more than the most expensive and comprehensive levels of breakdown cover.

Whether it is worth having the recovery service is another matter. Most breakdowns are dealt with at the roadside but with modern cars having so many electronic systems, often out of necessity to comply with strict emission regulations, the chances of something happening that can only be fixed by a garage are increasing.

Choosing how to buy

You've now worked out what you need and can afford to buy and run, which means you can research the models that meet your criteria. You now have to choose whether to buy new or used. If your budget is low, you may be forced to buy used, but even if you can afford new, you might not want to.

Here are the pros and cons:

Buying new pros	Buying new cons
The cachet of owning a new car	Dearer to buy
You can choose what extras to have	Heavy depreciation in the first year
You choose colour and trim	You bear the full cost of options which do not add to the trade-in value

Buying new pros	Buying new cons
You do not risk buying someone else's problems	You only get back part of what you paid for other options
You know the car hasn't been abused	Insurance is dearer
It has a long warranty	
It smells new, not of someone else	
You are more likely to get special offers and finance deals	

Buying used pros	Buying used cons
You avoid the first year depreciation	You may be buying other people's problems and mess
Cheaper to buy	Doesn't have the cachet of a new car
Cheaper to insure	Shorter warranty (if you get one at all)
You don't have to run it in	If it is old you must allow for costly repairs
	Finance deals are rare
	You don't know if it has been abused
	Its history must be checked

The next two chapters cover these two ways of buying.

10 THINGS TO REMEMBER

1   *Choose a size of car that suits your needs but do not go on external size alone because many small cars are roomy.*

2   *Choose an engine that suits your type of driving: a small engine may not be so economical for someone who does lots of motorway driving.*

3   *Diesels are more expensive to buy but have better fuel consumption and are kinder to the environment.*

4   *If you have strong environmental views, research the issue properly: biofuels and petrol-electric hybrid cars are not necessarily the greenest options.*

5   *The newer the car, the cleaner its engine will be. Running an old car does not help the environment.*

6   *Safety items like airbags and electronic driving aids are well worth having.*

7   *If you have children, a car with Isofix mounting points allows you to use safer child seats.*

8   *Get to know what your chosen model has as standard and what the extras are.*

9   *Check you can afford insurance before buying the car and always look at what policies include when making price comparisons.*

10 *Do not buy a car just because you were offered a good deal: you must live with it long after the money you saved has been forgotten.*

2

....

Buying new cars

In this chapter you will learn:
- *how to choose extras*
- *where to buy*
- *how to get the best from a test drive*
- *how to haggle*.

Buying a new car is the dream way of buying a car. Collecting a brand new car is a great feeling and you can largely configure it to suit you. You also have the reassurance of new cars coming with three-year warranties (five in some cases) so you can be fairly sure there will be no unexpected bills unless you break something.

If you already own a car and are deciding whether to trade-in or sell it privately, please see Chapter 12 on disposing of your car.

Show me the money!

Obviously, we'd all like to be able to buy a new car for cash. It is usually the cheapest way to buy, but even if you have enough money in the bank to buy a new Range Rover, don't entirely ignore finance. From time to time car dealers are able to offer finance deals where you either pay no interest for one to three years or you pay half the cost of the car now and the other half at some time in the future. If you have the cash, this is like giving you free money because even half the price of a cheap new car sitting in a high interest account somewhere can raise a substantial return – maybe enough to pay for a service.

There are five main ways of paying for a car:

- ▶ *cash*
- ▶ *personal loan*
- ▶ *hire purchase (HP)*
- ▶ *personal contract purchase (PCP)*
- ▶ *leasing.*

CASH

If you are paying cash, or a deposit on a car bought on finance, check what form of payment is acceptable to the dealer. If you pay by cheque they are unlikely to part with the car until the cheque has cleared. Banknotes will probably be acceptable for a few thousand pounds, but mean you will have to travel to the dealership carrying a substantial amount of money. A bankers' draft is usually acceptable, though for a substantial amount they may only accept one if they can check its validity with your bank. Some dealerships will accept a debit card payment, at least for deposits, but check whether your card has a limit and ensure the money is cleared if you have paid it in from somewhere else. Few, if any, car dealers accept credit card payment for a car because of the amount the card company charges them.

LOAN

There are an amazing number of firms you can get a personal loan from, ranging from high street banks to supermarkets, so shop around for the lowest interest. The best deals should rival HP (see below) and have the advantage that the car is yours from the beginning. Naturally, the lender can chase bad debtors through the courts, but they can't repossess the car. More importantly, if you want to sell the car before the loan is paid up, you can, which gives you greater flexibility in case your circumstances change.

HIRE PURCHASE (HP)

HP is the easiest to understand. As the name suggests you are
effectively hiring the car while you buy it and, even though it will be
registered in your name, it belongs to the finance company until you
have paid the debt. This makes it easier to get the loan because it is
secured against the car, so if you don't pay up they can come and take
it back. However, if you want to sell the car before the loan is finished,
the finance company will want to be paid off first and will probably
still want the interest they were owed. They also usually want a bigger
deposit than with other loans and monthly payments are higher than
for a PCP (see below). Zero interest finance is usually HP.

PERSONAL CONTRACT PURCHASE (PCP)

The PCP is the newest form of car finance. Like HP, the car
remains the finance company's until the loan is paid so there are
the same pros and cons. The way it works is you pay a deposit,
then monthly payments and at the end of the loan there is a lump
sum final payment, which may be called the minimum future value
or balloon payment. The great thing about it is that it brings lower
monthly payments than a loan or HP, bringing a new or nearly
new car more easily into reach. The lump sum may not sound
so clever, but you only have to find it if you want to buy the car
outright, which means you tie less capital up in it.

A PCP gives you three choices at the end of the term:

1 *Just give the car back.*
2 *Buy it outright.*
3 *Trade it in for another.*

The final payment is set at a level the finance company thinks will
be less than the value of the car, so the only time it would pay to
just give it back is if the company got it very wrong. Buying the
car outright means finding the lump sum, and over the whole term
this usually makes PCPs more expensive than HP, though if you
can get a good deal selling the car privately it may be worthwhile.

Most people want to trade-in and then the car will be valued in the normal way and any difference between its trade-in value and the final sum becomes at least part of your deposit on the new car. So, if the final sum is £3,000 and the car is worth £5,000, the dealer will send £3,000 to the finance company, so he knows the loan is paid off, and put £2,000 against your new car.

One criticism of PCPs when they first started was that they would tie you in to one car make, but that is no longer so. Most car franchises offer them now, as do some banks, so they are all used to paying each other's final sums.

One thing to avoid when negotiating a PCP is reducing monthly payments by increasing the final sum. This eats into the difference between the sum and the car's value, reducing the money you have as a deposit on the next car. PCPs can also include service costs and even tyres, though check carefully that it is worth it: there is no point paying extra for tyre cover if your mileage is so low you are unlikely to need to replace them during the loan term.

LEASING

Self-employed people registered for VAT may find leasing a car is a viable option because they can claim back the VAT on the lease payments and, usually, offset the rest against Income Tax. However, that depends on your circumstances and should be discussed with your financial advisor and car-leasing specialists. Leasing may also make sense for non-VAT registered people, if they can afford the higher monthly costs, because when you add depreciation to the cost of HP or a loan, leasing fees usually work out cheaper.

ARRANGING FINANCE

Most dealers have a specialist in the showroom, usually called a **business manager,** who is trained to explain the options and arrange finance for you. Many dealers have arrangements with an independent finance company as well as the car manufacturer's own finance house so they can see who has the best deal for you.

But remember that banks and other finance houses also do HP and PCP, so it may also be worth looking to them.

However, a car dealer gets a commission on setting up finance so, while a bank may set a lower interest rate, the dealer may offset that with a better discount on the car, because he can make up the money in commission.

BEWARE ADD-ONS

Look out for unnecessary add-ons to finance. Most try to sell you instalment protection insurance to cover payments in case of redundancy, which may be useless if you are self-employed or have someone who will bail you out. The UK's finance watchdog has also criticized its cost. Many offer guaranteed asset protection (GAP) insurance to cover the gap between finance owed and the likely insurance payout if the car is written off or stolen in the first year, which you don't need if it is already included in your car insurance (see previous chapter).

Insight

A car dealer with a sense of loyalty to customers once warned me of a common ploy finance houses use if you have turned down these extras. A few days after signing the deal, as he predicted, the finance house sent proposal forms for payment protection cover and GAP insurance, which they obviously hoped we would mistake for papers that must be signed for the finance. If you read them carefully you could see what they were, but they did not go out of their way to make it clear this was something you had already turned down and which had no bearing on getting finance.

CREDIT WORTHINESS

If you are not on the electoral register you may have trouble getting a loan because it is the first thing the credit-checking companies look at to see who you are. If you get turned down for finance by several companies, and can think of no reason for it, check your references with the main credit-checking companies Experian and **HPI** Equifax (it can be done online) and complain about anything that is incorrect. Your Citizens' Advice Bureau or bank may be able to help with this.

Insight

Most countries have something like the UK's Data Protection Act which gives you the right to know and correct information held on you on computer. It pays to check your rights before going after such data so you know what to insist on. Not all companies who hold data on you are as willing as the larger ones to comply with your rights unless you make it clear you know what they are.

Where to buy

European Union rules have changed so manufacturers can no longer force you to buy new cars from franchised dealers. Manufacturers already had less control over dealers in the USA and Australia.

FRANCHISED VS NON-FRANCHISED

Franchised pros	Franchised cons
Have the approval and backing of the manufacturer	Manufacturers can dictate whether discounts are given
Are vetted and trained by the manufacturer	
Offer a full range of after-sales services	
Have access to the whole network's stocks	
Are likely to get quicker delivery from manufacturers	
Know the cars	

Non-franchised pros	Non-franchised cons
May be able to offer bigger discounts	Up to you to check their credentials
Some are former franchised dealers so know the cars	Don't have access to large stocks of cars
Some can source finance from a wider range of firms	Have little influence if deliveries are delayed
	Rarely offer after-sales facilities
	May source cars from abroad (e.g. Japan) with specifications different from UK models

Franchised dealers

For most buyers, the franchised dealer is the easiest route. But don't just go to the one you pass on the way to work. You may buy a car in a neighbouring town but you can always get it serviced near the office (though don't say that to the dealer you're haggling with). Phone round to see what other dealers in the area have in stock and what deals they can do. This will also give you an idea of which dealers are likely to go the extra mile to get your custom and which can't be bothered.

DISTANCE

Distance from the nearest dealership to your home shouldn't be ignored. Many people say it doesn't matter because cars now have such long service intervals that you only need to visit the dealer once a year, and most do collection and delivery. In addition, you no longer have to have a franchised dealer service the car to keep the warranty valid, it must only be done to their standards. However, when you want accessories or parts or urgently need to get a small warranty repair done before you go on holiday, the distance starts to tell.

Non-franchised

If you buy from firms other than a franchised dealer, check what you are getting. Does it have the full manufacturer's warranty? If it is sold as a 'personal import', is it to UK specification? For example, Japanese specification cars have the steering wheel on the right but might not have the same equipment as UK models so it may not be as good a deal as it at first appears. Is it pre-registered? If it is registered to the company selling it, it should be substantially cheaper because it is effectively a used car. Be careful about handing large deposits over to companies you don't know and can't see and certainly don't pay up front in full.

You will find non-franchised dealers advertising on the web, in national newspapers and car magazines. You may find local dealerships doing it, often former franchises for the marque.

Pick your moment

If you can, arrange to visit showrooms during the week because the staff will have much more time to deal with you than at weekends.

If a dealer has the car you want in his showroom it reduces waiting time and means he may be prepared to give a better deal because he has no work to do to get the car. But for some highly desirable cars, or unusual colours or specifications, there will always be a wait, so get some idea of how long it is before committing yourself.

Shopping list

You have done your research so have some idea what you want. If there are extras you want in the car make at least a mental list of what you consider essential and what you can live without.

This way, if the dealer has a car in stock that doesn't have your desired factory-fit item you can quickly decide whether you will take the car or wait for one to be ordered with that item.

FACTORY FIT VS DEALER FIT

It is important to know the difference between factory-fit and dealer-fit extras. Factory-fit items are things that must be installed during construction, including interior trim, electronic driving aids and air conditioning. Dealer-fit items are things that can be installed by the dealer's workshops, like towbars, mudflaps and side steps on off-roaders. Some things can be both, like front foglamps, alarms and, on some cars, sunroofs. This means it doesn't matter if the car in stock doesn't have mudflaps because the dealer can fit them, but if it doesn't have air conditioning you'll have to wait. You are also more likely to get dealer-fit options thrown in because the actual cost to the dealer is much less than you would pay.

FUTURE COST OF EXTRAS

Don't go mad on extras because with most of them you will get little of their cost back when you sell the car on. However, there are certain extras that add to the value of the car at trade-in time (though even with those you will not get the full cost back).

Value-adding extras include:

▶ *air conditioning*
▶ *most automatic gearboxes*
▶ *good leather upholstery*
▶ *metallic paint*
▶ *satellite navigation on luxury cars*
▶ *alloy wheels on cars with steel ones.*

Money-losing extras include:

▶ *differently styled alloy wheels on cars with alloys*
▶ *upgraded audio*

- *different interior trims*
- *high tech equipment on modest cars*
- *safety equipment.*

However, safety equipment might save your life, which makes it worth the financial loss.

CHANGING ATTITUDES

Despite the above, attitudes do change. Satellite navigation was initially a financial loss but now is reckoned to add a substantial premium to luxury cars at trade-in. There is still some resistance to built-in systems from buyers of more mundane used cars, because they never trust advanced technology, but that may change as more people understand what it is. Laws prohibiting the use of mobile phones on the move may make options like Bluetooth wireless hands free connection more desirable.

Top tip

Before buying Bluetooth as an extra, check what you are getting. Not all in-car Bluetooth gives full access to the phone's address book.

COLOURS

Special paints like **metallic, micatallic** and **pearlescent** often pay and will at least make the car easier to sell, though so will a good strong, but not quirky, non-metallic colour. Colour choice is important because it does affect the value when you sell the car.

Black, silver, blue and red are safe colours. Take care with brighter colours because a bright red hatch would be in great demand but the colour might be a problem on a large luxury saloon. White is unpopular in the UK and odd colours, like grass green, bright pink, lilac or the catarrh-shade of metallic yellow that Fiat once tried are unwise. Some buyers think these are fun colours, but dealers know that to sell the vivid green hatch after trade-in they have to find

another person with similar taste and they are not as numerous as
potential buyers for black or silver cars.

The test drive

Before you waste your time, and the salesperson's, by taking a test
drive, have a good look at the car in the showroom and try and get
comfortable in the driver's seat. Dealers don't generally mind you
doing this as long as you don't have uncontrolled children leaping
around inside a brand new, unregistered car. Take time to check
the boot, ask someone to show you how to lower the seats and any
special features of the car.

Don't just sit in the car, adjust the driver's seat and the steering
wheel to get a comfortable position (see Chapter 4). If you can't
get comfortable in it, there is no point going for a test drive, but
get someone to show you the available adjustments so you don't
miss any. As well as a sliding seat with rake adjustable backrest,
even modest modern cars may have adjusters for seat height,
lumbar support pressure and steering wheel tilt. You may also
find adjusters for cushion angle, steering wheel reach, thigh
support and lateral support. Some luxury cars allow you to
vary the height of the lumbar support or even the shape of the
backrest.

Once you have a comfortable position, get in the back and see
if your passengers will have enough room behind you. As we've
already discussed, sunroofs can steal crucial headroom for a tall
driver but in some models they also cramp tall passengers in the
back because the roof lining may be lowered to give room for the
panel to slide back.

If you now think the car is for you, it is time to take or book a test drive. Don't expect to be able to walk in off the street and demand a test drive, especially if you want to try an automatic or a specific engine. It pays to ring in advance and set up a testing time because the dealer is likely to have a couple of key versions in a model range but not every one, and even those he has may have already been committed to something or someone else.

Top tip

Taking a drive in a higher specification model that is mechanically the same is fine, as long as you check the model you are buying has essentials like seat height adjusters if you are tall. But don't test drive, say, a 1.6 when you are buying the 1.4 or a manual if you want an automatic because you won't get a true impression of your intended car.

TESTING TIMES

If you book in advance, some dealers even offer test drive loans, subject to insurance, allowing you to try the car for a day or even a weekend, though this is usually restricted to luxury marques. At the other extreme, some may expect you to be satisfied with literally going round the block, but make it clear you expect more than that if you are going to buy the car because this is your only opportunity to see if it suits you.

Don't be intimidated by driving with a stranger: car salespeople are used to sitting next to all sorts of drivers, some of whom they would rather not trust their lives to. However, if you don't like the idea of driving through a crowded part of town in a car you don't know, ask the salesperson to drive it somewhere quieter before you take over.

GET FAMILIAR

When you first get into the car, get yourself comfortable and adjust all the mirrors so you can see properly. The salesperson should give you a run down on where all the controls are: listen even if you think it is the same as your own car because things may have changed on a new model. Pay particular attention to things you may need quickly – discovering you can't find the horn as someone starts pulling out into you or you can't wash the windscreen when a lorry spatters mud across it is not funny in an unfamiliar car.

So, check the positions and operation of:

- ► *lights*
- ► *horn*
- ► *wipers*
- ► *washers*
- ► *rear wash-wipe*
- ► *door handle*
- ► *window buttons or winder.*

MOVING OFF

When you are ready, check your surroundings, indicate and move off. Give yourself time to get used to the feel of the car. In the back of your mind, try to be aware of what it is doing while you are driving. Ask yourself:

1 *Are any of the controls heavier or lighter than I like?*
2 *Can I reach everything?*
3 *Can I see out well enough?*
4 *Can I live with the quality and volume of mechanical, wind or road noise?*
5 *Is the gear-change easy?*
6 *Am I constantly changing gear or is it flexible enough for my driving style?*

7 *Is the ride comfortable?*
8 *Does its handling inspire confidence?*
9 *Am I still comfortable?*

Basically, you have to decide if you can live with it. The difficult thing is deciding what you will get used to and what is likely to become more irritating. In general, you will get used to things being in different positions but high noise levels can become tiring. It can depend on your use of the car. For example, a boot released only by a lever next to the driver's seat will be no problem for someone who rarely carries much baggage but a real source of irritation for a regular shopper as they struggle to stop bags toppling over while they open the driver's door, release the lever and then lug everything round the back.

Insight

If you find something, like a boot release, irritating, mention it to the salesperson in case the car offers more than one way of doing something. A friend once complained that she had struggled for months with an internal boot release on her Peugeot before discovering that the car had a boot release button incorporated into the zero of the model number badge on the boot lid. It just goes to show, she should have read the handbook!

ROAD SENSE

Make sure the test drive includes all the types of roads you drive on most. If you do a lot of motorway work you want the chance to cruise at steady speed at least on a dual carriageway. If you live in the country you need something that feels good on twisting roads and can cope with humps and dips. If you only do town driving, these things won't matter so much but you will need something in which you feel confident when driving though crowded streets and that copes with stop–start traffic.

Change your style

If you are driving a diesel or an automatic for the first time, remember to adjust your driving style and seek advice from the salesperson. With most diesels there is little point revving them hard to get the best performance, like you would a petrol: you change up early to make the best of their pulling power by keeping them around 2,000 rpm. An automatic that doesn't change down for more performance when you want it may need a more positive foot on the pedal to bring the kick-down facility into play. If it has a sport mode or manual touch change, try those, too.

AND FINALLY

If more than one person is going to drive the car, make sure they have a go too. If the salesperson doesn't offer to leave you alone when you get back to the showroom, ask them to so the two of you can discuss your feelings about the car and decide if there is anything else you want to add to your options list or take off it.

Just a small matter of tactics: play down your feelings for the car. If you rave about it, the salesperson knows they don't have to try too hard to sell it, but if you underplay it they may be more flexible. Saying 'Well, I liked the leather seats but they seem very cold,' might get the heated versions thrown in. But this is where the negotiation starts.

Haggling

If you think haggling is impolite, just think of it as negotiation that is part of everyday life for the salesperson. As long as you go about it in a reasonable and calm way, they will not be offended and may even find it fun. In any case, a car salesperson is a trained negotiator so should be better at it than you.

Top tip

Customers who don't ask, don't get: if you are prepared to pay whatever it says on the windscreen, dealers won't refuse your money. Obviously, salespeople want to get the maximum profit for the dealership but they also want to sell cars so they are prepared to reduce their profits to do that.

GETTING TO KNOW YOU

A skilled salesperson starts with meet and greet, usually giving you a name and saying what position they hold. They're doing that to make you feel welcome and show that they are friendly, so it pays to do the same back: the salesperson who feels you are a pleasant person to do business with is more likely to offer a good deal.

The next stage is to qualify you as a customer. They'll chat about what you do, family, hobbies, where you live and any special needs you have for the car. There are several reasons for doing this, including wanting to see if you are serious customer, but a good salesperson doesn't want to sell you a car that doesn't meet your needs because they know you won't come back and may not even go through with the purchase if you realize the car is not for you. However, they may also be trying to see if they can steer you towards a more expensive model or one they have in stock, which is no bad thing if it suits you.

There's no harm giving this information and playing the same game back to establish rapport, but if you are asked what your bottom line is on cost, either suggest a figure that is slightly less than you can afford or make a flippant remark like 'As little as I have to spend'.

STARTING THE DEAL

If you already have a good quote from another garage, use it as a starting point because they will try to at least match it.

Tell them:

- *what extras and accessories you want*
- *if you want finance*
- *if you have a trade-in.*

They should then be able to make an offer, either as an all-in price or telling you how much you would need to pay on top of your trade-in.

If you are trading-in you can approach the offer from two angles: that you were expecting more for your old car, and/or you had hoped they were expecting less for the new one. You can throw a bargaining chip their way by saying something like you really wanted one with one of the extras, but at this price you can't afford it. That gives them the opportunity to offer to include the extra in the price or do a deal on the item, like fitting a towbar and not charging for the labour.

Keep calm and remember negotiation is about give and take. Use extras as bargaining chips, for example conceding that expecting them to throw in air conditioning was unfair, but how about metallic paint?

Eventually you will get to a position where they won't budge on price, but it is still worth trying to get a few cheaper things like floor mats and mudflaps if you can – and don't forget a full tank of fuel and a year road tax instead of six months. That said, six months tax may save you from converging bills in a year's time when a first service will be due, along with insurance if you have started a new policy on buying the car.

Top tip

If your salesperson has to keep running off to consult a superior on everything, politely suggest talking direct to that person, making it clear you are doing this to save everyone's time, not because you dislike dealing with a minion.

Discounts

How much should you get off? That depends on what and when you are buying.

Poor deals

The profit margins on cheap cars are very small – a few hundred pounds in some cases – so don't expect much. You are also unlikely to get discounts on very new models or cars in big demand and certainly won't get one on anything for which there is a waiting list. In America, dealers may charge more than list price for cars in high demand. If a dealer is doing money-off deals, you are unlikely to get extra discounts.

Big deals

You should get substantial reductions on soon-to-be-replaced models. However, check you are not saving a few hundred on list price when next year's version has, as standard, the air conditioning you are paying extra for. Models that are in over-supply may also come in for big discounts, though it may not be obvious which these are. You may get a little extra off if the dealer is arranging the finance because of the commission on it.

Seasonal

Choosing your time of year can help, too. In the UK we have two annual number plate changes that create big increases in sales, so you might do better at other times of year unless you are after nearly new cars (dealers tend to change demonstrators when new plates come in).

Christmas and New Year is slow for car sales so you stand a better chance of a discount, though a January car is worth more than a December car when you trade it in because that month means it's viewed as being a year younger.

At certain times of year, usually around October and November, some dealers offer good deals on pre-registered cars. These are cars the dealer has registered but not sold so they have delivery mileage only, like a new car, but are technically used cars because they are registered to the dealer. The main reason dealers do this is that the car companies give them bonuses for meeting or exceeding certain sales levels and if they are close to those levels it is worth them registering a few cars to sell at discounts because the bonus is more than the discounts. You may even get these cars at the equivalent of trade price or as if VAT has been dropped.

CLOSING THE DEAL

Once you have agreed a price, you can discuss how you are going to pay and when you can collect the car. Try to get a confirmed delivery date so you can put pressure on if they do not deliver on time. Make sure the dealer has your correctly spelled name and full address for the registration documents because it saves having to correct them later.

What happens next?

Once your car is delivered to the dealer it will be registered and given a **pre-delivery inspection (PDI)** to make sure everything has been screwed together properly and it has suffered no transit damage. The dealer will tell you the registration number, so you can insure it and then provide a valid certificate of insurance for the dealer to tax the car. Some insurers will send the certificate direct to a dealer, though it is better to get them to send it to you so you know that you have it and can then take it to the dealer.

We will look at delivery and your first few days with the car in Chapter 4.

10 THINGS TO REMEMBER

1 *Even if you can pay cash for a car, check dealers' finance offers in case they are offering interest-free deals.*

2 *Find out whether you can get better finance through your bank.*

3 *Check finance add-ons like payment protection and GAP insurance are valid for you and not already covered by existing insurance or available more cheaply.*

4 *If possible, seek deals from more than one dealer for the marque, not just your local one.*

5 *Visit dealers during the week, if you can, when they are not so busy.*

6 *Before taking a test drive, check the car over and make sure it suits you. There is no point taking a drive in a car you do not feel happy with in the showroom.*

7 *Think carefully before adding lots of extras because you will not get the money back when you sell the car.*

8 *Choose colours carefully: quirky ones may affect future value.*

9 *Take a test drive on the sorts of roads you use.*

10 *Stay calm and reasonable when haggling prices down.*

3

Buying used cars

In this chapter you will learn:
* *how to buy a used car*
* *where to buy from*
* *how to minimize the risk*
* *where to get professional help.*

Buying a used car has a lot of advantages beyond just being cheaper than a new car, though it does have pitfalls for the unwary.

Finding finance is the same as for new cars unless you are buying privately or at an auction, in which case a personal loan is your only option (see Chapter 2).

VAT on cars

In the UK you pay Value Added Tax on the retail price of a new car and any accessories and services (so you pay tax on the costs of, say, a towbar and the fitting charges). Once the car becomes a used car, if it is sold on by a dealer, VAT is only charged on their profit on the deal. In practice, dealers write off that small amount of VAT in the deal. It becomes more complicated with commercial vehicles, which includes things like four-door pickups and 12-seater versions of the long wheelbase Land Rover Defender stationwagon, which are legally minibuses. With these, businesses

(Contd)

can claim back the VAT so if the first owner was VAT registered, the tax has effectively not been paid on the vehicle, so the next owner is charged VAT on the used price. Where this gets complicated is that if the previous owner or the person selling a used one is not VAT registered, the tax is deemed to have been paid, so on subsequent sales it should be charged in the same way as on a used car. If you feel someone is charging VAT when they shouldn't, tell the local Customs and Excise.

Know your car

Whoever you choose to buy a car from, do your homework. Make sure you know what was standard and what wasn't in the model you are after at the time it was registered so you don't find out too late that equipment you really wanted didn't become standard until the following year.

Before you start a serious search, take a look at the adverts in local newspapers, used car small ad magazines and online used car websites to get an idea of what price cars are being advertised for. Age, mileage and condition are all factors affecting a car's value. The first two are almost always given in an advert, though take vendors' assurances of condition with a pinch of salt – that's something you have to assess when you view the car. As explained in Chapter 2, most extras do not usually add value to a car so if someone selling a car which had alloy wheels as standard expects more because it has special ones fitted, they are indulging in wishful thinking. However, things like automatic gearboxes, air conditioning where it is not standard and, on upmarket cars, satellite navigation, do add value, but nothing like what they would cost on a new car.

There are publications available at any newsagent listing used car prices, most allowing you to make adjustments for mileage. Some used car websites offer valuations, and Glass's (the people who publish the used car price guide used by many dealers) offer an online valuation service at www.glass.co.uk for a small fee. A printout of the Glass's valuation could be a useful negotiating aid when it comes to haggling prices.

IS IT CARED FOR?

One thing you often see in car adverts is that it has a full service record or history. This is important because it proves the car has been serviced according to the manufacturer's schedule and should give an indication of whether the mileage is genuine. Manufacturers' warranties require that servicing is done to schedule so it is particularly important if it still has any new car warranty to run. It may simply take the form of a garage stamp in the handbook or a special service book but it is much better if it is backed up with receipts which will also show what was replaced and when. Don't worry if a car has been up to 1,000 miles or a month late for a few services, most manufacturers accept that sort of delay, but think twice if one has been very late or missed.

If someone has done DIY servicing, which is common on older cars, they should still have receipts for parts like oil filters and, if they knew what they were doing, they would have kept a record of what was done. If they can't prove it, you have to ask yourself if the car is worth the risk that it wasn't done properly or at all.

When the car is yours, keep up this service record because it will help make it easier to sell on and get a good price for.

Find your car

There are so many ways of finding used cars that buyers are now spoiled for choice.

Websites are very useful ways of finding used cars, whoever you plan to buy one from, because they make finding cars that meet your criteria so easy.

If you plan to buy a specific marque from a dealer, look at either your local dealer's website or the national site for the car maker (they're probably linked). Almost all now have used car searches with dealer sites, showing what they have in stock and what they can get through the rest of the network.

While some general used car sites are online only, some are linked to publications, whether specialist used car small ad magazines or local newspaper groups. The great advantage of these sites over paper publications is that you do not have to hunt through column after column of adverts because the computer does that for you.

Most used car websites have multiple search criteria where you can enter the type, make or model of car, price range, engine sizes and fuels, age, gearbox type and how far you want to travel. Some are better than others and the best allow you to register your criteria so the site emails you when a suitable car comes in, though it is still a good idea to check the site occasionally in case something slips through. Some websites show both private and dealer cars.

Top tip

When entering price criteria put in more than you can pay – you can haggle prices down and you don't want to miss cars advertised at just a little over your maximum.

TRADITIONAL

If you do not have internet access, turn to the traditional advertising media. Local newspapers are a good starting point because they carry adverts placed by both private and trade sellers, though the former may tend to be at the cheaper end of the scale.

Specialist car small ad magazines offer a wider range of private and trade sellers and some, like *Autotrader*, have regional editions so you do not have to wade through adverts for cars hundreds of miles away.

Used cars advertised in national newspapers and magazines tend to be at the top end of the market, or specialist vehicles, like classic cars.

At the other end of the scale, the card in the newsagent's window is a good place to find old bangers. Look out for signs in car windows, too.

Your rights

Before looking at where to buy, let's look at how that affects your rights as a purchaser. These rights vary considerably in different countries, so please check locally.

The UK's trading laws give you considerably more protection when you buy from a dealer, of any sort, than when you buy privately or at auctions, including those online. You can get up-to-date information on your rights through leaflets at your local Trading Standards office (usually a county council responsibility) or at the Trading Standards Institute's website at www.tradingstandards.gov.uk, which also has a search facility for finding your local office.

Your rights are enshrined in the **Sale of Goods Act** and vendors can't remove these rights by using phrases like 'sold as seen'. A warranty must be in addition to those rights and not attempt to replace them. For example, they can't force you to accept a repair if you are entitled to replacement.

TRADERS

When you buy from a 'trader', which can be anything from a franchised dealer to a man who regularly sells cars from his home, the car must be of satisfactory quality, as described and fit for purpose. The last includes any special purpose you make known to the vendor, like being able to tow or carry a certain weight. The law doesn't define 'satisfactory quality' and with a used car its age, mileage, price, description and 'all relevant circumstances' are taken into consideration. That is because you would not expect the same from a high mileage five-year-old car as you would from a low mileage two-year-old car. Even so, the law requires that, unless sold for scrap, it must be roadworthy, capable of passing an **MOT** and reasonably reliable.

PRIVATE SALES

If you buy from a private individual your only protection is that the car must be of the quality described, so make sure you keep all documents relating to the sale, including the advert. Even then, enforcing your rights against an individual can be difficult.

FAULTY GOODS

If it is faulty or not as described, whoever you bought it from, the law says you only have a 'short time' to reject it and get your money back. What qualifies as a short time varies from case to case but if the car is so bad you want to reject it, stop using it straight away and inform the vendor and your finance company. Trading Standards suggests getting legal advice. If you accept a repair you do not lose your right to reject it later.

If you fall outside a 'short time' you can demand replacement or repair. If the car is replaced, the vendor is entitled to an allowance for the use you've had of it, though you can demand compensation for inconvenience. Under consumer law, if a car suffers a fault within six months of purchase, the trader has to prove the fault was not there when he sold it. But you have to provide evidence to support a claim and, especially if it goes to court, a vehicle inspector's report might be useful.

AUCTIONS

You have least protection at auctions because they are not legally consumer sales so you are bound by the auction's written rules. Some are better than others, with the worst being little more than a warning that the buyer must beware.

ADVICE

Your local Trading Standards office and Citizens' Advice Bureau give general consumer advice and the latter can usually suggest local solicitors who can handle claims. If your complaint is with a franchised dealer, contact the car manufacturer's customer service department or the **Society of Motor Manufacturers and Traders (SMMT)** on 020 7235 7000 or at www.smmt.co.uk/consumeradvice. If a garage is a member of the **Retail Motor Industry Federation (RMIF)**, they offer an arbitration arrangement through the National Conciliation and Arbitration Service. Contact the RMIF on 020 7580 9122 or at www.rmif.co.uk. The **Scottish Motor Trade Association (SMTA)** also has a conciliation service and can be contacted on 0131 331 5510 or via www.smta.co.uk.

Insight

Even if you are satisfied with your 'new' used car, keep all the documentation related to it, including the advert, because you never know what may happen in the future. Also keep a note of private vendors' names, addresses and phone numbers. When I've sold cars I have been shocked by how trusting people have been. The last one didn't even want to look under the bonnet: he just assumed that because the car was externally clean, it would be mechanically fine. I even had to persuade him to look at the registration document to see it was ours to sell. No matter how trustworthy someone seems, you do not know them and may be giving them a substantial amount of money. If it turns out your trust was unjustified, you want justice and recompense.

Franchised dealers

The safest way of buying a used car is generally through a
franchised dealer. Many people will tell you they always charge
more than independent dealers, but they do get the pick of the
crop, particularly with their own marque. Indeed, franchised
dealers increasingly only sell the same marque as their new car
franchise, often selling on other makes either to other dealers or
to the dealership in their group that specializes in that make. If
you are looking for an unusual model or a fairly recent one, the
franchised dealer may be the only place to find one.

APPROVED WARRANTIES

Some dealers charge more than an independent dealer might for the
same car but almost all franchised dealers sell used cars with their
manufacturer's approved used car warranty. The value of the benefits
in these warranties can be several hundred pounds, so if you compare
prices with an independent dealer you must take this into account. An
independent may offer a warranty, but does it come to this standard?
In addition, an approved used warranty is recognized at any of that
make's dealers so if you buy it in Penzance and move to Peterborough
or break down in Perthshire, you still get the same backup.

Approved used warranties require that a car complies with certain
standards in the first place, like age, mileage and having a verifiable
service record. It then lays down the level of preparation it must have,
including a history check, and then covers it with a comprehensive
warranty that includes breakdown cover. Some even include Europe-
wide breakdown cover and MOT failure insurance – many are even
close to the manufacturer's new car warranty.

The usual cover is for a minimum of one year. This means if it is
a one-year-old car with two years of the new car warranty to run,
you get that. If it is two and a half years old you get the remaining
six months of the new car warranty and six months of the used car
one; if it is three years old you get a year of the used car warranty.

The other thing about buying a used car from a dealer specializing in that marque is that if someone has traded-in, say, a Toyota for another Toyota you can assume they were happy with it. If it had been a problem car, they would have chosen another make.

Finally, there is the peace of mind. The dealer is a specialist in that marque so is familiar with all its service needs and any manufacturer recalls or notices about it. As well as having the protection of consumer law, there is the watchful eye of the manufacturer who has set down minimum standards for its dealers and has a disputes procedure for when something goes wrong, mediating between customer and dealer. It should be remembered, though, that with few exceptions your local dealer is owned by someone other than the manufacturer – they are entirely separate businesses.

Insight

Most franchised dealers also have the ability to search their network's entire used car stock but if one says they can do that for a 'search fee', politely refuse. The chances are they will use exactly the same search that is available to you, free, on the manufacturer's website. But do not expect them to get a car for you from a long way off unless you are fairly certain you want it or are prepared to pay a fee for their time and transport costs, which is fairly safe on cars backed with a manufacturer approved warranty.

Independent dealers

These can range from upmarket specialists in quality cars through dependable village garages to a couple of blokes operating out of a scruffy backstreet lot. Some specialize in certain types, like ex-fleet cars, 4×4s or performance cars. The quality of the cars and the standard of service can be equally varied, so ask around to find out what sort of reputation they have locally.

Whatever they are like, you have exactly the same protection in consumer law as when buying from a franchised dealer, but with a backstreet fly-by-night it could be a lot harder to enforce it. Choose a dealer with a good reputation and you shouldn't have any problems because they want to keep that reputation and build up business by word of mouth.

WARRANTIES

Those specializing in really cheap, ageing cars usually do not offer warranties beyond saying that if anything goes wrong within a certain time you should bring it back (see 'Your rights' earlier in the chapter). Some may offer a warranty for extra cost, but before you buy these, demand to see the warranty document and read what you are getting. Some are so vague and hedged around with get out clauses that they literally are not worth the paper they are printed on. Those backed by motoring organizations, the Retail Motor Industry Federation (RMIF) or Scottish Motor Trade Association's (SMTA) Scotsure are among the reliable ones. Many have different levels of cover, so check which level is being included.

It is best to get a warranty that is backed by a third party rather than just by the dealer because if the dealer goes out of business, or refuses to comply with the warranty, you have someone to go to. These warranties also allow you to make a claim if you get the repair done elsewhere, just like making an insurance claim. Incidentally, third party warranties always come with some sort of printed 'receipt' or insurance schedule either handed over at the time or sent later stating that a fee for a certain level of cover has been paid – make sure you get it because the warranty is invalid without it.

PREPARATION

Ask what preparation the car will get. Most independent dealers, to protect themselves, run a history check on the car and do a mechanical check. Many, to save problems later, will, as a matter of course on older cars, replace the **timing belt** (sometimes called a **cambelt**) which drives the **camshafts** which operate the engine's intake and exhaust valves. These belts must be replaced at mileages laid down by manufacturers, usually above 60,000 miles, and if they break it can result in serious and expensive damage.

Some dealers give the car its next service early, but others only do that if it is due in less than a couple of months. Dealers usually get a new MOT done, regardless of how long the existing one has to run. Some sell a car only with the remaining road tax but it is more common for dealers to do that only if it has a long period to run, like more than six months. A few may include a new one-year tax disc and there is no reason why they shouldn't because they can get a refund on the old one.

If the car is still showing signs of previous occupation, ask if it will be given a full valet before delivery. That said, why buy a car that reeks of dogs or cigarettes when there are plenty that don't?

CREDIT WORTHY

Any used car dealer who is not licensed for credit is probably suspect because it means finance houses don't trust him. This means used car dealers can offer at least hire purchase, though the interest rates may not be as good as franchised dealers with their big buying power and manufacturer-backed finance. Some may even be able to arrange PCPs on newer cars (see the finance section in Chapter 2).

Dealers who are members of the RMIF and SMTA have to comply with a code of conduct and minimum standards set by these trade organizations.

Private vendors

The advantage of buying from a private vendor through the small ads is that you should get more car for your money, though you need to have the cash or arrange your own loan. A car sold this way should go for something between what the vendor would have got for it on trade-in and what a dealer would have sold the used car for. Some price guides quote a private sale price, but for those that don't, it is a simple enough sum to do yourself.

However, as explained in the 'Your rights' section above, you get far less protection when buying privately than buying through a dealer. The majority of people selling cars this way are decent, ordinary folk who just want to get the best price for their car, but the trouble is that the dishonest ones look the same. It is up to you to ensure that the car and the vendor are all they seem.

Top tip

Don't be afraid of offending people because it is your money at risk. If someone takes offence at you wanting to avoid leaving yourself open, just explain politely that you don't know each other and there is a lot of money at risk and while you're sure they're honest you have no way of knowing that for certain. If they continue to make a fuss, work on the principle of 'the lady doth protest too much' and find another car.

RESEARCH

As always, do your homework so you know what you are getting and have some idea of what that model of that age has. It is not unknown for private vendors to put the GLX badge on the cheaper LX model and hope you won't notice the lack of velour upholstery and electric windows.

TAKE A WITNESS

It is always wise to take someone with you when seeing privately sold cars. Apart from providing you with a witness, and a second pair of eyes and ears to spot discrepancies, there is the safety aspect of going to meet someone you don't know on their ground when they can reasonably assume you at least have the money for a deposit.

DODGY DEALERS

The worst dishonest vendor you can get involved with is the dodgy dealer who sells cars while pretending to be a private individual.

The only reason for doing this is to rob buyers of their legal rights which automatically means you are dealing with a dishonest person selling cars they have no faith in. So, when you reply to adverts, don't say 'I'm ringing about the Golf GTI you have advertised in the *Free Press*...' but instead say 'I'm ringing about the car you're selling...'. A genuine private seller is unlikely to have more than one car advertised so will know you are talking about the Golf GTI in the *Free Press*, but a dodgy dealer would have to ask which car you mean or where it was advertised.

PHONING HOME?

Be very wary of people who only give a mobile number or who give a land line and mobile but the former is never answered regardless of what time of day you call (it could be a phonebox). With pay-as-you-go mobiles it is far too easy for someone to sell a bad car, or steal your money, and then disappear leaving no way of tracing them.

Similarly, take care when dealing with someone who gives a land line phone number but asks that you only call at certain times. It may be someone who doesn't want people ringing before they get home from work or calling so late they wake the kids, but it could also be someone using a payphone, though you should hear a distinctive bleeping when it is answered. After all, with answering machines and services so freely available, why would anyone not want you ringing during the day?

Even more suspicious, is someone who gives a mobile number or call time and wants to meet you away from their home. If they say the car is in a lockup garage, suggest you meet at their home and they can take you there. If someone is honest they shouldn't mind doing this but if they refuse, just forget the car because you have no way of tracing the vendor.

DO THEY KNOW IT?

A genuine owner should know the car and how everything works and not have to look for the bonnet release or spare wheel. They should know when they bought it, where to find the service record in the handbook and how much MOT and tax it has left. They should also be able to show you the registration document and various bills relating to the car.

No matter how much you want a particular car, if there is anything that strikes you as odd about the vendor, car or the circumstances, it is safer to walk away. There will always be another one. No matter how trustworthy someone seems, always ask for proof. If they say it has just had several hundred pounds' worth of work to get it through an MOT, they should be able to show you the bills and an MOT certificate. They should also be able to show proof of ownership, a service record and all the other documents associated with car ownership.

PAYING

It is reasonable for the vendor to ask for a deposit of a few hundred pounds to show your good intent while you get the rest of the money. If you are paying cash it is also safer to do it this way rather than to go looking at cars, and meeting people you don't know, with pockets full of money. Remember, though, to get a written receipt saying what you have paid and what the full price is. If you are getting a vehicle inspection or history check, the receipt should say this is to be refunded if the car fails.

Agree with the vendor how the rest of the money is to be paid. Cash is easiest but has the drawback of vulnerability to theft. Certainly, don't let the person take the money away to count it because it would be too easy for them to abscond or pocket a few hundred and say the sum is short. A cheque is safer but it is reasonable for the vendor not to part with the car until it has cleared, though special arrangements can be made with some banks. Probably the safest way for both parties is a banker's draft which guarantees the vendor that the money is there and means you can take the car and its documents straight away, though it is best to check it with the issuing bank first.

Auctions

Auctions are best left to the experts. Some try to look after private buyers more than others, but in general they are geared towards the trade. These trade buyers know how much to pay, what to look for and what they can repair at a reasonable price, yet even they sometimes make mistakes.

As explained in the 'Your rights' section earlier, you have little protection under consumer law. In addition, you have to be able to bid based on a visual inspection of the car, though if the vendor has warranted it in some way the sales rules may allow you a test drive before handing over the money.

You should get a car for a lot less than you would any other way as long as you don't get carried away with the bidding, which many trade auction veterans say private buyers always do. At an auction, you take the risk that it could cost you more in the long run, so don't blow your entire budget on the car in case it needs repairs. It is also wise to go to a few auctions to see what happens before you go along to bid, and you need to find out what payment methods are acceptable to the auction house. Make sure you can also get a car home that may be untaxed and uninsured.

Online auctions bear the same risks as a physical one, with the same limited consumer protection and the added risk that you don't see the car before bidding. Read the site's conditions of use very carefully.

What to check

When viewing used cars, make a checklist of the following points:

Outside
▶ *Is it as described?*
▶ *General condition outside*

- ▶ *Tyres*
- ▶ *Lights*
- ▶ *Note registration number*
- ▶ *Note VIN if shown on windscreen*
- ▶ *Check tax disc date and registration number*

Inside

- ▶ *State of the interior*
- ▶ *Do doors unlock and open properly?*
- ▶ *Do electrical items work?*
- ▶ *Wipers*
- ▶ *Seatbelts*
- ▶ *Seat adjusters*
- ▶ *Note mileage*
- ▶ *Look for VIN under carpet flaps*

Under bonnet

- ▶ *Find VIN and engine number if visible*
- ▶ *Look for leaks*
- ▶ *Check oil*
- ▶ *Check fluid levels (see Chapter 5)*
- ▶ *Is the engine cold?*

Paperwork

- ▶ *Does the registration document show the vendor's name?*
- ▶ *Do the numbers on it tally with those on the car?*
- ▶ *Is the MOT valid?*
- ▶ *Does the MOT mileage tally with the car's?*
- ▶ *Does the vendor's insurance cover you to test drive?*
- ▶ *Does your insurance cover a test drive?*

Test drive

- ▶ *Does it start properly?*
- ▶ *Was there any smoke?*
- ▶ *Does it tick over properly?*

- *If the vendor is driving, is he familiar with it?*
- *Gear change*
- *Clutch*
- *Brakes*
- *Steering*
- *Performance*
- *Comfort*
- *Visibility*
- *Any odd noises?*
- *Allow to idle then blip throttle: any smoke?*

The deal
- *Note agreed price*
- *Receipt for deposit*
- *Agree payment method*
- *How much road tax included?*

Be prepared

Don't arrange to go and see a car in the dark because you will never get a good impression of its condition under streetlights or in a poorly lit garage. Ideally, choose a dry day because raindrops can hide the condition of the paintwork.

Don't wear smart clothes and take overalls with you if you have them – you are going to need to kneel on the ground and feel around under dirty wheel arches and in grubby engine bays. Take a small torch and tyre tread depth gauge with you. People used to say take a magnet to check body panels for filler but modern cars have so many plastic and aluminium panels that this is pretty pointless now.

If you are meeting a private vendor, leave a note at home of who and where they are and when you expect to be back.

Appearance

Have a look at the general condition of the car. Does it look right for the mileage? You would not expect a low mileage car to have badly scuffed paintwork, a shiny steering wheel and gear-knob and badly worn carpets.

Does it look as if it has been cared for? Someone who can't be bothered to empty the ashtrays and get the banana skins out from under the seat to sell it, probably hasn't been too careful with it the rest of the time. Don't be too put off by surface dirt, though it can hide paintwork faults. Even grubby seats will come clean, but damage and ground-in dirt, inside or out, are much harder and more costly to put right.

Is there any obvious crash repair work? Properly carried out crash repairs should not show at all so it hasn't been done well if you can see paint overspray on door and window seals or signs of rippled panels on the outside. A common sign of poor repairs is where easily visible panels are replaced or done reasonably well but those underneath are not. For example, an external wing panel has been replaced but the wheel arch under the bonnet has been left or botched with filler, or when you lift the boot carpet the floor still shows deformations. This is not just a cosmetic problem because if the structure of the car has been put out of alignment the car may not handle properly and in a crash the body of the car may not provide the level of protection it should.

Check all the tyres, including the spare. They should be legal and show no signs of uneven wear (see Chapter 6 on tyres) and if you're buying from a dealer you should be able to haggle into the price the replacement of tyres with less than 4 mm of tread.

UNDER THE BONNET

In the engine bay, touch the engine to make sure it is cold: if someone has run it before you got there it may have cold starting problems.

Look for signs of leaks, including fresh marks on the drive. On a very old car a greasy look to the engine is not unusual, but shiny oil patches may suggest trouble. Water leaks may not show wet on a cold engine because the cooling system is not under pressure, but you should still see signs of where the water has sprayed and dried. Look for deposits like mayonnaise under the oil filler cap and in the coolant expansion bottle (don't take the top off this if it is hot or you could get scalded). This is where oil and water have emulsified together suggesting that an engine **gasket** has gone allowing coolant and oil to mix, which requires expensive work.

GET INSIDE

Do the doors unlock and open without graunching? This is simple maintenance anyone can do with an oil can so it could suggest neglect.

Does everything work? Check the operation of lights, stereo and anything electric, including seat adjusters and belts, the heater fan, windows, wipers and mirrors. You can't check a heated rear screen works, unless you can get the windows steamed up, but have a look for scratches on the element.

CLOCKING

Modern digital odometers are difficult to tamper with (known as 'clocking' in the trade) and some even display error messages if someone tries, but it is not impossible and leaves no physical evidence.

Old fashioned odometers with the numbers on rotating drums are easier to clock but it is also easier to spot clumsy attempts. Look for signs that the instruments have been removed, like damaged screw heads or misaligned dials, and for marks alongside the numbers where someone has turned the drums. Many people say to look for numbers not lining up, but it's normal for them to be out of line for some time before and after a big change, like going from 9,999 to 10,000.

Note the figure shown for later checking.

Test drive

If you buy from a dealer you can take a test drive just as you would with a new car. If you buy privately, you must check the insurance situation. If the vendor's policy covers all drivers comprehensively, you have no problem. Think twice about driving it if your policy only covers you for third party for other people's cars because if you have an accident you could end up paying to replace someone else's car. Most comprehensive policies are only comprehensive on the insured car (see the insurance section in Chapter 1).

If you can't drive it, at least get the vendor to take you for a ride in it so you can see what it goes like and sounds like.

Top tip

Be careful about driving off with a stranger, especially if you are alone and female. If you have any doubts about them, say you'll come back later with a friend. It may be wise to call someone and let them know you are taking a test drive: you can always claim you are letting someone know you might be late. If you text someone with this information, add the car's registration number.

WHAT TO LOOK FOR

As well as all the things you need to check in a new car test drive, as explained in the previous chapter, you want to be aware of whether the car shows signs of problems.

- *Does it start easily and run smoothly?*
- *Does it smoke? Some older diesels may give a puff of pale smoke on starting from cold but it should soon clear.*
- *Does it track straight or pull to one side?*
- *Does the steering feel right or does it feel too slack?*
- *Do the brakes work well? (Only test them on a safe, straight road with nobody behind you.) Does the gear-change feel right?*

- ▶ *Does the clutch do everything in the last few centimetres of travel? That could mean expensive clutch replacement.*
- ▶ *Are there any odd noises from anywhere?*

When you finish, sit in the car for a few minutes with the engine running then blip the throttle and check for smoke. If it belches smoke, that may suggest engine wear.

It is worth doing all these things even if you are getting a vehicle inspection by an expert because if you spot anything untoward you could save yourself the expense of calling in the experts. However, it might be worth a call to a garage or motoring organization for advice on how serious anything you find really is. You would be daft to lose a good car for the sake of a £50 repair.

If you find anything that needs putting right, either insist the vendor gets it done before the sale or find out how much it will cost and get that knocked off the price. The former is the best way of avoiding nasty surprises if the garage finds more work is needed than expected.

Paperwork

If you buy from a franchised or good independent dealer they will almost certainly show you documentation to prove how the car has been checked. Have a good look at it all. There should be something to show they ran it through a history check to make sure it is not stolen, written off, subject to finance or a hire car. They are likely to have a tick-box check list (which doesn't actually prove the items have been checked) and records of servicing.

With a private vendor ask to see documents *after* you have seen the car, so you can first note from the car the registration, Vehicle Identification Number (VIN or chassis number) and, if you can find it, the engine number. VIN is always shown on a plate somewhere in the engine bay but you may also find it stamped in the floor somewhere near a front seat (often under a lift up section of carpet) or, on most modern cars, on a plate visible through the base of the windscreen. On off-roaders with a separate chassis, you may find it stamped into a chassis rail under one of the wheel arches. The engine number is stamped somewhere on the engine, but is often hard to see, especially on modern cars where the engine itself is often barely visible under all the plumbing, electronics and acoustic covers. You need to check these tally with the documents you are shown and you need them to run a history check (see next section).

TEST CERTIFICATE

In the UK, if the car is over three years old it must have a valid annual MOT test certificate. The design of these changes from time to time but they always carry the car's registration and VIN numbers and the name and address of the test centre.

Unfortunately, garages do get burgled for blank MOT certificates so there are false ones about but you can check its authenticity on the Vehicle Operator Services Agency's helpline on 0870 3300 444. MOT certificates have been computerized since May 2006, with details kept on a **VOSA** database, so you can also check them online at www.motinfo.gov.uk.

Incidentally, no roadworthiness test is proof of current condition: it simply means the car was roadworthy on the day it was tested. For example, a tyre might have had 0.4 mm more tread than required by law when tested a month ago, but 0.5 mm could easily have worn off since, so it would now be illegal.

Insight

One thing I would never do is to accept a car that has less than a month to run on its MOT. The vendor might offer to pay for the test but the MOT is your only evidence of roadworthiness and you must suspect that someone who couldn't be bothered to get it done before selling the car may know it would not have passed. You have no guarantee they will keep promises to pay for repairs once you own the car. Worse, it may have already failed an MOT. You can get a car tested up to a month before the certificate runs out, but if it fails, that failure goes on the computer record and renders the previous MOT invalid. This is so that a dangerous car cannot be driven away from a test centre on the basis of an 11-month-old test with one month still left to run.

MILEAGE

Some registration documents and all MOT certificates show the vehicle's mileage, so check that the odometer (mileage reading) shows a reasonable amount of use since the paperwork was done. Wise owners keep all their MOT certificates as evidence that mileage is genuine. So, if the paperwork suggests the car has only done 5,000 miles in the past year (half the average motorist's mileage) you need to ask why. There may be a genuine reason, like it being a second car only used for short trips or the owner has been abroad, but it could also suggest tampering.

History checks

It is odd that few people would buy a house without getting lawyers to check its legal standing and surveyors to see whether it will stay standing, yet when it comes to our second biggest purchase, many rely on luck and their own limited knowledge. At the very least you should get a history check, especially when buying privately, to ensure there is nothing untoward known about the car. The firms who carry out history checks on used cars say about one in five are shown to be suspect, so the risk of buying trouble is high.

If you buy from a dealer it is likely they will already have had a check run on the car to protect themselves, so they should be able to show you a printout of what was revealed. Some manufacturer-approved used car warranties include a history certificate in the car's warranty documentation. However, if you are buying privately, get the check done: you can always do it from your mobile or ask the vendor to let you use their land line so they won't have to wait long. If anyone objects, you have to wonder why.

History checks are not expensive but they give you peace of mind and a comeback if they are not what they seem.

WHO DOES THEM?

These checks are carried out in the UK by the two big data handling companies, HPI Equifax and Experian, though they may be marketed by other people like the AA and RAC. HPI have an online service at www.hpicheck.com or you can do it by phone on 0845 3008905 or through the RAC on 0800 9755867 or at www.rac.co.uk. Experian's checks are offered to the general public through the AA at www.aacheck.com. Fees vary and there are discounts for members of the motoring organizations. Some online used car websites also offer discounted checks through these firms from time-to-time.

Both companies back their checks with compensation if anything later proves incorrect, and both issue certificates showing what information has been found out about the car.

HOW THE CHECKS ARE DONE

To get a check you need the car's registration, VIN and, preferably, an engine number. You also need to know the exact make, model, engine type, year of registration and colour so you'll know if any of these do not tally with what the check reveals.

The checks against a database show whether the car:

- *is recorded stolen*
- *is subject to finance (with some credit schemes it belongs to the finance company)*
- *is a 'high risk' vehicle like a hire car*
- *has been written-off by insurers*
- *has had a number plate change.*

WRITE-OFFS

If a car has been written-off by an insurer it means they believed it could not be economically repaired. There are four levels of write-off and in the three worst cases a **Vehicle Identification Check (VIC)** notification is flagged up against it with the Driver and Vehicle Licensing Agency. If anyone tries to register the car the **DVLA** will not issue documents until an identity check has been carried out by the Vehicle Operator Services Agency. That is hassle you can do without.

PLATE CHANGES

A plate change is normally something innocent like a previous owner having had a cherished plate on it that they want on their new car, but it can be a way of trying to cover a dodgy history, so further checks are done.

Vehicle inspections

A vehicle inspection by an expert is the ultimate peace of mind, though it is likely to cost a few hundred pounds. Prices usually vary according to how thorough a check you want and the age and value of the car. The easiest way to get them is through your motoring organization but you can also look in the Yellow Pages under vehicle engineers.

Most vehicle inspections start with a history check and if it throws up anything, you only pay for that. Inspectors generally give a verbal report, so you immediately know if there is anything to worry about, and follow that with a written report. They usually explain the severity of any faults and give some idea of the likely cost of repair.

You can use this report either to get the vendor to have the repairs done (ask for proof) or to get the likely cost taken off the car. With serious faults the former action is best in case it costs more than the inspector's estimate and to ensure the car is safe to drive. With minor ones, it may be better to haggle the price.

If someone objects to waiting while an inspection is done, even though the organizations do them as quickly as possible, you should question why. Do they know that it has problems? If someone pulls the old 'I've got other people interested and I can sell it by tomorrow evening' call their bluff. For all they know, the other would-be buyers might want the same as you and the vendor has you showing an interest now. Why should you be pressured into putting your money at risk because a stranger wants a quick sale or is frightened that faults will be revealed? However, it is reasonable that they ask for a deposit to confirm your interest, though you need a receipt saying it is refundable if the car fails the inspection.

Hand it over

If you buy from a dealer they will be familiar with change of ownership documentation and look after it all for you. If you buy privately you and the vendor should carefully read the registration document to make sure you have filled in everything you need to and both signed the relevant places.

REGISTRATION

The current UK registration document is a multi-coloured form with a pink section at the bottom of page three explaining what you must do if the car is sold privately. The first five sections give information about the car and owners. You or the vendor need to fill in the green sections (6 and 10) with your name, address and age. Section 6 has space for your driver's licence number and the car's current mileage, neither of which are legally necessary but they provide protection for you, the vendor and future owners.

The thing many people forget is that section 8 must be signed by both the vendor and the buyer. The vendor then sends everything as far as section 8 to the Driver and Vehicle Licensing Agency (DVLA) and gives you the tear-off section 10 which says on the back how long it should take for the new registration document to be sent to you and who to contact if it isn't. The vendor should keep the pink section at the bottom of the page, which tells him what happens next and who to contact if it doesn't. It is important to both of you to get this right – if you don't the car is not officially yours and the previous owner is still liable for taxing it and for speeding and parking fines and congestion charges.

The green section 10 is now your only proof of ownership, but only an idiot would leave it at that.

RECEIPTS

Get the vendor to write a dated receipt saying what you have paid, giving both your names and addresses and stating what the car is, including age, mileage, make, model and engine. It speeds things up if you tell the vendor you'll want this when you leave a deposit, so they can prepare it in advance. This gives you evidence that you have paid in full and who you have paid it to, while giving them a record of who they have sold it to.

If the car is more than three years old, the vendor must give you a valid MOT certificate. Make sure it has the correct tax disc, too.

Safe keeping

If you haven't already done so, when you get home create a file somewhere safe in which to keep all the car's documentation. Include the advert for the car as evidence of how it was described by the vendor in case something goes wrong. If all the ownership documents, insurance paperwork, MOT certificates and service bills are in one place it makes life easier. For example, when you tax the car you will need the insurance certificate and MOT and if you make an insurance claim they might verify the date of first registration and ask for the date of the last MOT. As we've seen, MOT certificates and service bills all help when you sell the car on, so it is worth keeping them. In addition, many garages guarantee replacement parts they fit for six months or a year, so you need to keep the bills for at least that long.

10 THINGS TO REMEMBER

1 *Find out as much as possible about the car you seek.*

2 *Check features you think essential were fitted to a model of the age you are considering.*

3 *Seek cars with service histories.*

4 *Keep the advert for the car in case you need it as evidence of how it was described.*

5 *When you phone a private seller about a car, say you are calling 'about the car you're selling' because a true private seller will know straight away what it is.*

6 *When buying from a dealer, ask for evidence that the car has had a status check.*

7 *If buying from a private seller, at least get a status check done on it yourself.*

8 *Always seek proof of everything, don't just take a stranger's word that it is theirs to sell, the mileage is genuine, maintenance has been done and the MOT is valid.*

9 *Avoid viewing cars in the dark, in the rain or alone.*

10 *Get a receipt stating the car and vendor's details and make sure you both fill in the registration document properly.*

4

The first days

In this chapter you will learn:
- *about taking delivery of your car*
- *how to get to know your car*
- *how to run it in.*

You are now the proud owner of a new car, or at least one that is new to you. For most people taking delivery of a car is a time of great excitement tinged with a little fear because it would be awful to damage it on your first drive. You can reduce that risk by taking delivery at a time when the roads are not too busy and then by giving yourself a little time to familiarize yourself with its controls, just as explained in the test drive section in the previous chapters.

Dealer handover

If you bought the car from a dealer, especially if it is brand new, they should run a handover procedure which can take anything from a few minutes on a basic car to an hour on a high tech luxury one. There are two reasons dealers do this: it covers them if you do something stupid, like turning the lights off because you thought that was the wipers, and because too many people can't be bothered to read a handbook.

Listen to what you are told, because as well as explaining the car's systems, they should explain things necessary to comply with the warranty, like whether there is an inspection after a few hundred miles. With complex cars, concentrate on the driving controls because you can always read up on the stereo or satellite navigation later. Also pay attention to anything they say about the layout of the handbook and where it is kept – many cars now have a special compartment in the glovebox or elsewhere for the handbook. It might also be useful on the way home to know where the spare wheel and tools are kept.

While you are being shown over the car look out for anything untoward. It is unlikely you will spot anything they won't, but if you do you can get it sorted before taking delivery. If your deal included a full tank of fuel, take note of whether the gauge registers as full when they turn the ignition on to show you things.

The dealer will also hand over important documents about the car's ownership, warranty and finance as well as key and radio security codes. Keep all this safe and not in the car, otherwise you hand a thief 'proof' of ownership, the means to get duplicate keys and to render a stolen radio usable.

Insight

While I always stress 'read the handbook' some manufacturers do not make it easy. Increasingly, they make special holders for the book, not all of which are entirely obvious. For example, some Mercedes-Benz have a purpose designed handbook cubby inside the fold down armrest between the back seats, while many cars have slots for the book in the roof of the glovebox, which can only be seen with your head on the passenger seat. So, make sure the vendor shows you where it it is located.

Finding fault

When you buy from a garage they should conduct a pre-delivery inspection to make sure everything is in order. Even a new car can have faults – either things missed at the factory or damage done in transit to the dealer. But a car is a large and complex beast so things get missed and sometimes a technician concentrating on important safety related items may miss something more trivial, like ill-fitting trim.

So, your first action when you get the car home is to have a thorough look over it. This will also allow you to familiarize yourself with it, so keep the handbook ready in case you need to look up how something works or how to get access to parts of the car.

We're not talking about a mechanical examination here. Just look for damaged trim, things not fitted properly, marks on the seats, paint scratches and leaks. Check windows, seatbelts and locks work properly, that folding seats fold and latch back when you return them and make sure everything that should move, does.

Top tip

It is very common with new cars that nuts and bolts dropped by factory workers are found under the lift-up back seat cushion or in the spare wheel well and while these do not constitute a fault they may rattle around and make you think there is something wrong. If you find any, keep them in case they have fallen out of where they should be.

If you find faults, contact the dealer straight away. If you bought the car privately it is probably only worth trying to get the vendor to do anything about it if it is serious, and even then it might not be worth the hassle. Whoever you are talking to, be polite because, especially in the case of a dealer, if they knew the problem was there they would have done something about it. However, be firm about getting it put right. If the car must have an early inspection after a few hundred miles you can leave minor faults until then but seek the dealer's guidance and remember that to put it right they may need to order parts, so must know in advance.

Light reading

Car companies spend a lot of time creating handbooks and complain that too few owners read them and therefore many 'faults' are remedied by telling the owner what page it's on. Time reading the car's handbook is not wasted. It enables you to get the best from your investment by using its systems properly and tells you how to care for it. Everything in the rest of this book should be read in conjunction with the handbook because we can't explain everything for every car and your model may have unique or recently developed features.

Take something as simple as folding the rear seat. The whole seat may be split in sections, or just the back. The cushion may have to be tilted forwards before folding the back, it may drop down automatically with the back or it might be fixed. If the cushion lifts, you may have to release a catch, lift it at the front first or simply pull the back edge up. The seatback might be released with buttons on its top edge that push in or pull out or there may be a lever to pull somewhere else on the seat or even near the tailgate or side door and any of these releases may be lockable. It might fold with the head restraints in place or you might have to remove them before folding it and if you do there may be special stowage for them. All this is explained in the handbook yet service departments speak of people who have broken seat releases by forcing them the wrong way because that's the way they went in their old car.

Insight

A friend who hadn't read her handbook complained to me that it was 'bad design' in her new Volkswagen that she had to turn on the electronic stability programme every time she started the car. I had to point out she was actually turning it off every time she started the car. She then read the handbook and found there were a number of other bits of 'bad design' that were really driver ignorance, like thinking it lacked a boot light when it was simply switched off.

SAFETY FIRST

Handbooks also give information important for your safety. Not only do they tell you how to use safety systems, but they flag up any potential risks that might damage you or the car. These range from the obvious, like keeping hands out of the spinning cooling fan, to the not

86

so obvious like not putting stickers over airbag positions, which can seriously affect their deployment. Knowing how to use the child locks on the back doors could merely save you the embarrassment of not being able to get out of your own car or it could save your child's life.

MEMORY AID

Handbooks have to cover a whole model range and it can help to cross out sections not relevant to your car, like bits about diesels when you have a petrol or stereos different to that fitted in yours. You don't have to learn it by heart, just take in the important stuff and make yourself aware of what is in there so that if, say, you have to change a wheel you'll know there was something about locking wheel nuts to look up.

Don't expect to remember all the functions on complex audio or navigation equipment. What works for many people, with any complex equipment, is to read the handbook, use the device for a while to familiarize yourself with the basic operations, then read the book again. On the second reading you will have more idea of how it works so can take in the more advanced features.

It can help to sit in the car while you read because you can confirm the locations of switches, explore how something works and when you find something that can be programmed to suit your preferences you can do it then and there.

Finding your way

Unfortunately, we can't guide you through the handbook because there are too many formats. Most modern ones are sensibly laid out in obvious sections with important safety information at the front. But in some, especially those on older Asian-built cars, the layout and English leave a lot to be desired.

Some handbooks have an easy to find page giving 'forecourt information' like fuel grade, tyre pressures and lubricant types and volumes, but if yours hasn't then it may help to write the page numbers, especially for tyre pressures, on the cover.

Indexes can be pretty odd in some car handbooks, for example, one puts the location of the spare wheel under safety. It helps to remember American words and spellings because many Japanese handbooks index things like the bonnet release under 'hood' and tyres as 'tires'.

Driving position

Cars are sold worldwide so any car has to cater for all body shapes and sizes. Designers aim to accommodate the '98 percentile person' which means a comfortable driving position is possible for 98 per cent of us. If you are exceptionally tall, small, fat or thin you come in the remaining 2 per cent and may never get comfortable without adaptations. But the most average of people may never get comfortable if they do not use the adjustments properly.

SEAT ADJUSTERS

Modern cars have seats which slide and have rake adjustable backs, but adjustments for height, cushion angle and lumbar support are also increasingly common, with most cars also having at least tilt adjustment for the steering wheel. Luxury cars may also allow you to adjust the cushion length, side bolsters and upper and lower seatback angles, often electrically with memory to save settings for different people (see Plate 2).

Your handbook explains what is available in your car and how it works. For example, seat height adjustment may be by a lever you pull to unlock the seat and then allow it to rise or push down with your weight. Or it could also be a ratchet system where you push repeatedly down to lower or pull up to rise. Some cars now have a similar ratchet system for back rake.

While it is usually safe to make minor adjustments on the move with electric or manual ratchet systems, other seat mechanisms should only be used when parked, especially forward and aft adjusters that could allow you to slide away from the pedals.

Insight

If a car has electric seats with memory, I don't change the memory position when I make minor changes to the seat's position. Wait until you are sure the change is one you like. You can always revert to the original setup if the adjustment doesn't work for you after all. Also check whether the memory buttons work when the car is on the move (for safety, on a drive or in a car park). If they do, avoid fiddling with them while driving because if you hit the wrong button you could suddenly find the seat being adjusted to a position logged by someone much smaller or taller than you, which is not funny in the middle of a bend.

GETTING IT RIGHT

Seat specialists Recaro suggests eight points for a comfortable driving position, though some are only adjustable on the best seats.

1 *Start by pressing the base of your spine into contact with the back of the seat and then slide the seat until your knees are still slightly bent when the pedals (clutch on a manual, throttle on an auto) are fully depressed.*

2 *Press your shoulders firmly against the seat and set the back angle so you can reach the steering wheel with your elbows slightly bent. Your shoulders should still touch the seat when turning the wheel. In cars with reach adjustable wheels you can avoid sitting too upright or having to have a shorter leg length than is comfortable by moving the wheel.*

3 *Set the seat as high as possible to ensure a natural leg position and good view of the instruments and out of the car. Tall drivers may have to compromise here. A tilt-adjustable wheel can allow you to get a good view of the instruments without*

compromising your driving position, though with some cars tall drivers may find it impossible to see some of the binnacle without having the wheel uncomfortably high.

4   On seats where the cushion angle is adjustable, set it so you can depress the pedals easily and your thighs rest lightly on the cushion. When adjusting this you often have to readjust the seatback angle.

5   Head restraints are safety equipment and must be adjusted properly to work. They should be raised so their tops are at least level with your eyes (see Figure 4.1), though Recaro suggests it is best if it is level with the top of your head. On restraints where you can change the angle they should be tilted to about 2 cm from your head. Only if they are high enough will they protect you from potentially crippling **whiplash** injuries.

6   Recaro suggests that the ideal gap between the cushion, if adjustable for length, and the back of your knee is two or three fingers' width.

7   Adjustable lumbar support is correctly set when it supports the base of your spine in its natural position.

8   Adjustable side bolsters should support the upper body comfortably without undue pressure.

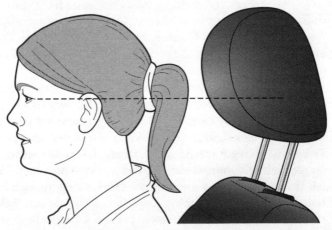

Figure 4.1 The top of the head restraint should be at least at eye level, preferably higher as shown here.

If you are used to driving in an incorrect position, one set up like this may feel odd at first but give it time and see if you are more comfortable.

Mirrors

Now you are comfy, adjust the mirrors so you can see in them. Electric mirrors make it easier and most switch from left to right either by sliding a switch across or twisting a joystick-style knob.

Top tip
> If you have short arms it is easier to adjust a passenger side manual mirror if a helper moves it for you.

Safety

More and more safety equipment is being built into cars and it is important to read up on it in the handbook. The positioning of things like airbags and child safety locks varies from car to car.

SEATBELTS

The most obvious safety features are seatbelts, whose use is now compulsory in most western countries. Only the very oldest cars are likely to have static belts which can be very awkward to adjust so that they are close enough to work but not to restrict movement. It may be wise to see if inertia reel belts can be fitted instead. Inertia reel belts roll in and out of a lower reel, which locks on sudden movement so they are largely self-adjusting, though heavily padded clothing can affect this.

Any seatbelt should pass the stress of impact on to your skeleton, not soft tissues, so the lower part must cross the hips and the diagonal should cross the sternum and collarbone (see Plate 3).

Figure 4.2 Pregnant women and larger people must pass the seat belt around the bump.

If your belly bulges, or you are pregnant (see Figure 4.2), the lower part must go below the bulge and the upper part must go round it. For women the diagonal passes between the breasts or severe bruising could result.

Modern cars have adjustable upper belt anchorages to help bring the diagonal to the right point on the collarbone. The handbook explains how to do this in your car, though some adjust automatically.

REAR SEATBELTS

In the back, most cars have inertia reel belts for the outer seats but they may be combined with either a static lap belt in the middle or another three-point inertia reel. A lap belt must go across the hips and be tight enough to stop you quickly without being uncomfortable as you sit. Some three-point centre belts unclip completely from the seat to allow it to fold. These have two buckles, which are sometimes colour-coded (see Plate 1). It's easier to work out which buckle goes where before anyone gets in the back – the one on the end of the belt goes in first, then the one that slides up and down is pulled across just like any other seatbelt.

Rear seatbelts not only protect the person sitting in the back but stop them flying into the people in the front. This is frequently fatal – at just 30 mph the average man hits the front seat as if he weighs the same as an elephant. Incidentally, if you are carrying heavy loads, it is safer to do up the rear belts if nobody is in the back because it supports the seat against the load in a crash (it also stops the buckles rattling).

Insight

I flatly refuse to carry any passenger who will not use a seatbelt. They may not mind the risk, but I do. In addition, if they are unbelted in the back they are a danger to those of us in the front who have chosen to be sensible. I've never had anyone decide to get out of the car rather than do up their belt.

AIRBAGS

As explained in Chapter 1, airbags are important safety features but can be dangerous if misused. Your car's handbook explains where they are in your model so you can avoid abusing them. Be particularly careful not to put objects over them, like mounting a mobile phone in front of one to become a missile if the bag goes off. Even a sticker in the wrong place can deflect an airbag from its life-saving path.

If you need a baby seat in the front seat, the car's handbook explains if and how you can disable the passenger airbag. This is usually done with a key operated switch which may be hidden. In cars with passenger airbags that can be disabled, there are two airbag warning

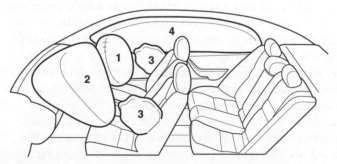

Figure 4.3 Typical airbag locations – 1 driver, 2 front passenger, 3 side, 4 curtain.

lights, one showing the bag has been disabled and the other showing there is a system fault, so be sure you know which is which.

CHILD SEATS

New cars have Isofix child seat fixing points (see Chapter 1) and your car's handbook will explain which of the car's seats they are on and how to use them. In some cars the lower ones are behind pop-out or hinged covers in the seats, usually marked with an anchor or child seat icon, in others you have to feel between the cushion and lower seatback to find the loops. The anchorages in the boot may be behind carpet cut-outs, but don't mistake load tie down points for them – check the handbook.

If your car has Isofix but your child seat isn't compatible, it is sensible to replace the seat because this fixing system is far safer. Non-Isofix seats install in a variety of ways so it is vital you read the manufacturer's instructions carefully. Since May 2008, all child seats in Europe have had to comply with the UN ECE 44.03 standard, which has been on sale for years.

You must also match the seat to the child. Children's body proportions change as they grow and with younger children their heads are proportionately much bigger than an adult's head. Because of this the support and protection children need changes as they grow: a baby is far more prone to neck injury, because of the size of its head in relation to its body, than a 12 year old.

In addition, a seatbelt has to pass stresses on to the skeleton, as described earlier for adults, and this is impossible to arrange without the help of a special child seat.

The correct seats are as follows (these are 'appropriate child restraints' in UK law):

- *Rear-facing baby seats: for children weighing up to 13 kg, which should see them to a year old.*
- *Forward-facing child seats: for those between 9 and 18 kg, which is between about nine months and four years old.*
- *Booster seats: for children weighing 15 kg and above, which means from about four years old.*
- *Booster cushions: for children weighing 22 kg or more, or about six years old.*

When you drive abroad with children, check local laws as there are considerable variations with some countries having minimum ages for children travelling in the front. In most countries, the driver is liable for prosecution if children are not safely restrained.

UK child seat laws

Children under three must use the correct child restraint (seat) in any vehicle. The only exception is in a taxi when a restraint is not available.

In vehicles with seatbelts, children must use an appropriate child restraint from the age of three until they are 135 cm (4 ft 5 in) tall. The only exceptions are:

- *in a taxi when a child restraint isn't available*
- *in 'an unexpected necessity' when one isn't available*
- *when two occupied child seats in the back of a car stop you installing another (it would be safer to use a proper child restraint in the front if there is no active airbag).*

You must not use a rear-facing baby seat in the front seat with an airbag unless it has been deactivated manually or automatically.

A UK Department for Transport pamphlet on child seats is available and can be downloaded from www.dft.gov.uk/think. Its safety advice should be followed in any country.

CHILD LOCKS

Child safety locks have been mandatory on cars with rear side doors for years. They usually take the form a tiny lever somewhere near the lock on the part of the door hidden when it is closed. Some cars have something like a screw head you can insert the end of a key into to turn so there is no chance of it being flipped by accident (see Plate 4). A few cars have electronic locks that can be activated with a switch in the front of the car.

When they are activated, they stop the rear doors being opened from inside for two reasons: first, children can open car doors deliberately or by accident and fall from them on the move, and second, they also mean a child can't open the door and rush out when it is unsafe to do so. But be sure to remember they are on because some adults panic if they can't open the door and exert extreme force on the handles. It is also embarrassing to ask a passer-by to let you out of your own car.

Starting

Many people think they know how to start a car so they skip that section in the handbook, but those who passed their tests before fuel-injection was commonplace, those switching to diesel and those with cars with security and starter safety devices, may have problems.

NO FEET

Modern cars' engine management systems supply precisely the amount of fuel required for starting so putting your foot on the throttle pedal while you turn the key, as you would with a **carburettor** system, messes this up. It could give starting problems and certainly wastes fuel with an environmental impact.

DIESELS

Diesels have a device called a **glowplug** which warms the **combustion chambers** to aid starting. You turn the ignition on and wait until a warning light with a symbol like a light bulb filament goes out before turning the key to start the engine, with your foot off the throttle. Glowplugs normally do their job quicker than you can fasten your seatbelt. It is an essential process when the engine is cold and failure to do it in very cold weather could result in the pistons pushing against unburned fuel and acting as hydraulic rams, which damages the engine. It is not so important on a hot engine so the latest technology sees the glowplugs and their warning light only come on when required.

Insight

There is a museum near my home with a collection of giant diesel engines once used to drive land drainage pumps. One has the equivalent of glowplugs, actually blowtorches aimed at large bolts, and a volunteer engineer told me that there is a record of someone trying to start one of these engines without using the 'glowplugs' properly. The pistons created so much hydraulic force with the unburned fuel oil that the cylinder head was lifted off the engine with such power that it demolished the end wall of the pumping house. 'That's why I always make sure I use the glowplugs on my car, no matter how warm the engine is,' the engineer said.

IMMOBILIZERS

Most cars today have engine immobilizers and a few cut in if you do not start the car within a short time of unlocking it. The car will not then start until you use the remote control to relock and unlock it, which you can do from inside. Immobilizers and alarms are usually only deactivated if you unlock the car with a remote control: they stay on if you use the key in the door.

TRANSMISSION SAFETY SWITCHES

All automatics have a gearbox safety switch which stops them starting unless they are in the park position, which locks the **transmission**, though some also start in neutral. A few manual gearbox cars, mostly from America and Korea, also have a safety switch on the clutch pedal so they only start with the pedal depressed. It is a good idea to do that anyway because it lessens the load on the starter by totally disengaging the engine from the transmission.

Warning lights

Warning lights come on with the ignition to show you they are working, then they should all go out except for the seatbelt one if someone's belt is not fastened and the lights for anything in use.

Your handbook explains what they are and when they should and should not come on. Generally, if it's red or orange, it's something serious, but never ignore any warning light. A few minutes spent checking what it means, and what you are advised to do, could save a lot of grief.

Insight

A former colleague was stupid enough to think it was better to drive 20 miles home with the oil pressure warning light on than to stop and check. Had he spent a few minutes doing that he would have realized the car was extremely low on oil which could have been topped up to get him home. Instead, the engine seized a few miles from home and he had

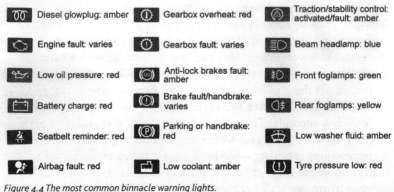

Figure 4.4 The most common binnacle warning lights.

to explain to the newspaper's fleet department why he had wrecked his company car. After that he was always given hand-me-down cars.

Security

Theft from cars and, of course, theft of them is a big problem, so car-makers build in increasing levels of security. But security devices are only any good if you use them properly. Read up on them in your car's handbook and remember they are all rendered useless if you 'give' the thief the key by leaving it in the car when you go into shops or to pay for fuel. You may only be in there for a minute, but it takes seconds for someone to start a car and drive off.

KEYS

Theft of keys is now the most common way for prestige cars to be stolen because their security is so good. This includes house breaking or simply lifting keys off a hall table by poking a stick through the letterbox. So, even if yours isn't a prestige car, guard the keys by putting them in a pocket, not on a desk or on a shop counter while you pay, and by keeping them safe at home, either in a drawer or on a hook in a cupboard. This also means visitors won't be able to see where they are and come back later.

Insight

Every time we have frosty weather there is a spate of car crime the insurers call 'frosting'. It is one thing to start the car's engine to run heaters and demisters while you scrape the ice off the windows, but it is madness to leave the car outside, running, with the keys in, while you go indoors, even for a few seconds. Thieves know people do this and may even have watched the street to see who does it regularly. Others may be opportunists who simply don't fancy walking to the station in the cold. If your car is stolen this way it is unlikely your insurance will cover its loss.

Many cars now have **transponder** chips in the keys which are interrogated by electronics in the car before engine immobilizers are turned off. If your car has these the key set may include a master key which is often a bright colour. This key should be kept safely at home because it is used to programme replacement keys and it will be extremely expensive to replace.

ALARMS

The best car alarms have movement sensors to detect intrusion in the passenger compartment. The handbook should tell you where the sensors are, so you don't put things in front of them, and how to disable them if you need to, for example if you leave a dog in the car or if something keeps setting them off. Many people fail to realize that you can't leave windows or sunroofs open with movement sensing alarms because they detect air movement. Flying insects inside the car, notably moths and lacewings, can set them off, so if you get false alarms look for insects on the windows.

Top tip

Think carefully before disabling an alarm: it could be a thief trying to get you to disable it by making it sound, perhaps by hitting the car.

PROGRAMMING SYSTEMS

A security feature often overlooked is the way many cars' remote central locking can be programmed to only open the driver's door on the first press of the button, opening the other doors on the second press. This stops someone leaping into the passenger side as the lone driver gets in. On some cars this is programmed by doing something to the remote sender while others have it on a multi-function screen in the car.

The programming may also offer the option for automatic door locking when pulling away. This means the doors lock above a certain speed so nobody can get in at the traffic lights or by forcing you to stop. Operating the interior handles overrides this and the systems either have impact sensors or are linked to the airbags to unlock the doors in an accident.

Keep your cool

Ventilation systems on cars have improved greatly over the years with even the most basic systems now offering fine control over how much air comes in and where it goes. Handbooks generally show this with lots of diagrams of where the hot and cool air goes on various settings. If you pay attention to these you'll get the best from the system, demisting windows efficiently and providing warm air without making the car stuffy.

MANUAL SYSTEMS

With manual systems you generally find that relatively small adjustments to temperature bring big results. So if you are too warm don't move the control all the way to cold but move it a little and give it time before making further adjustments. This way you can avoid constantly readjusting it as you drive and should achieve

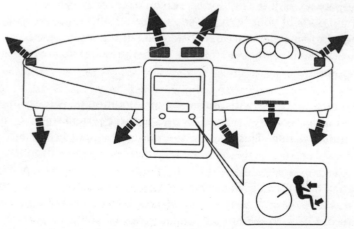

Figure 4.5 Handbooks often show where air goes on different ventilation settings.

a comfortable setting. You are simply balancing the controls against the temperature of the air coming into the car.

Some manual systems have simple push-button air conditioning. Many people complain these become 'too cold' even on the hottest day, but that is because they haven't understood that you take the chill off the air with the heater control.

AUTOMATIC SYSTEMS

Automatic systems, which are often called **climate control**, literally control the climate in your car for you (see Plate 5).

You tell it what temperature you want (20°C is usually comfortable in temperate climates) and it balances the hot or cold air to achieve it, regardless of outside temperature. If the outside temperature is high, it uses air conditioning to cool it down, but only if you have pressed the button to activate air con.

Fully automatic systems have an 'auto' button that handles everything including maintaining the chosen temperature, deciding on air distribution and running the fan. Some auto settings are so good you literally set the temperature and forget it, but others overboost it with the fan for no reason or try to freeze or fry certain parts of your body, so you are better off setting everything yourself. Some manufacturers offer semi-automatic systems which automatically maintain the temperature but you organize distribution.

A common mistake with automatic air conditioning is for people to get into a very hot or cold car and turn the system to the coldest or hottest setting. This doesn't cool the car down or heat it up any quicker, in exactly the same way that setting your oven to 200 degrees doesn't make it reach 180 quicker. To speed up heating or cooling, turn the fan up and use the recirculation setting so it is not trying to heat or cool incoming fresh air, but remember to turn it back to the normal intake setting or you'll sit in your personal fug and may get drowsy. Some automatic settings switch to recycling for themselves for the first few minutes.

Recirculation's other use is to stop fumes and bad smells getting into the car, so flip over to it if you are stuck behind a smoky vehicle or go through a badly ventilated tunnel.

YEAR ROUND USE

Air conditioning isn't just for the summer. You should use it at least once a month in the winter to keep it working properly and allow the refrigerant to circulate, which also protects the seals. But you'll find that if you use it when you need to demist windows they will clear quicker and stay clear no matter how dank it is outside. That is because, as the air is cooled, a lot of the water in it condenses out instead of being drawn into the car.

Don't be tempted to direct cold air at any part of the body because it can cause stiffness and muscle cramps. Sometimes you can create more diffused ventilation by directing side vents against the windows and middle ones up at the roof. In hot weather in some cars, directing conditioned air up the windscreen cools your head without a draft from a vent freezing your cheeks.

Top tip

Many people don't use air conditioning unless desperately hot because they overestimate its impact on fuel consumption. However, modern systems do not have as much of an impact as older ones, especially on powerful cars, and almost certainly have less effect than the drag caused by driving with the windows open.

KEEPING IT FRESH

Air conditioning systems need servicing and cleaning, otherwise moulds and bacteria build up in the refrigeration matrix creating smells, and the refrigerant may need topping up or changing. This may be done as part of the car's service but many garages offer air conditioning cleaning and servicing as a stand alone job if not, or if it gets smelly between services. It is not a DIY job because the refrigerant gas is under pressure and can cause serious injury if you open the wrong valve.

Any car made since 1990, and some older ones, is likely to have a cabin air filter. These filter out particles, like pollen, rubber dust from tyres and exhaust soot, and most have an activated carbon element to remove gaseous pollutants. These filters need replacing about every 20,000 miles or airflow is reduced and they can't protect your health. They are especially important for hayfever and asthma sufferers because on a car without a filter allergens do not leave the car at the same rate they get sucked in. So, check the filter is changed at services.

Fuel

The car's handbook, and sometimes a label near the fuel filler, says what type and grade of fuel you should use.

PETROL

Most petrol cars on the road now run on unleaded fuel and those with catalytic converters can only be run on it. Petrol with a lead substitute is still available on some forecourts for old cars which still need the additive to protect the engine's valve seats. Petrol has an **octane number** which signifies its grade, but in the UK is labelled Premium for 95 octane and Super for 98 octane. Most cars run on Premium and there is no point using a higher grade of petrol than your car requires because it does not improve performance. A few high performance cars do only give their maximum performance on Super, but these days most will also run on Premium and few drivers are likely to notice the difference.

BIOETHANOL

Bioethanol is a petrol alternative made from vegetable sources (see Chapter 2). If your car is capable of running on bioethanol, it will also run on petrol or any mix of the two. However, you can't use bioethanol in a petrol engine not adapted for it. Bioethanol cars therefore only need one fuel tank where dual-fuel cars have a conventional petrol tank plus an entirely separate one, with a special filler connection, for liquid petroleum gas.

DIESEL

Diesel has a **cetane number** but you don't need to know it because oil companies supply diesel with a higher cetane rating in the winter for easier running and to reduce the risk of 'waxing', where a wax-like substance forms in the oil at very low temperatures, clogging the system.

In Europe, most diesel is 'bio-diesel mix' where conventional diesel, derived from the same crude oil as petrol, is mixed with diesel obtained from vegetable sources, like oilseed rape. Diesel that is up to five per cent bio-fuel can be used in any diesel engine. It is low in sulphur and other impurities so, as well as making the exhaust cleaner, it seems to make diesels run smoother and, in many cars, results in a slight improvement in fuel consumption.

We may also be seeing pure bio-diesel more widely available with, hopefully, a considerable tax advantage because it is from renewable sources. However, pure bio-diesel cannot be used in all engines so you must check in the handbook or with your car's manufacturer to see if it is safe to use it.

Incidentally, don't be tempted to use tax-free oils like heating oil, vegetable oil or 'pink' agricultural diesel in your diesel car. To do so is illegal and though your diesel may run on them, heating and vegetable oil do not have the right additives to protect the engine and agricultural diesel dyes the fuel filter and pipes pink so the authorities can see you've used it.

Insight

I live in a rural area where the authorities regularly run roadside checks to catch people who have been using pink diesel in road vehicles. This is not done just to catch tax-dodging agricultural workers but because thousands of litres of diesel are being stolen from fuel tanks on farms, often by potentially violent intruders. If you are offered diesel on the cheap from suspect sources, refuse it or you may have awkward questions to answer if you get stopped.

The AA alone has around 100,000 calls a year to drivers who have put petrol into a diesel car. You shouldn't be able to do it the other way round, unless you have a very old car, because diesel pumps have a larger nozzle than unleaded petrol pumps. On old diesels you could get away with mixing a few litres of petrol with diesel as long as you topped up with diesel as soon as possible. But modern diesels' fuel injection operates at very high pressures using high speed fuel pumps and all this needs the full lubricating qualities of the oil which is diluted by petrol. So with a modern diesel, do not start it if you make this mistake: call your breakdown service because a wrecked fuel pump is extremely expensive to replace and warranties do not cover damage resulting from using the wrong fuel. (See Chapter 10 for more information.)

Running in

Even if your car manufacturer hasn't recommended a running in procedure on a new car, it is still wise to treat it with some consideration. The reason for this is to allow the machinery to bed in, though manufacturing tolerances on modern cars are so close that a lengthy running-in period is no longer necessary. That said, it is not unusual, especially for diesels, for the engine to use a little more oil than usual during the first few thousand miles. Indeed, there are certain circumstances in which a used car needs a running-in period, as we'll see.

Check your handbook for manufacturer's suggestions but the usual advice is that you avoid full throttle acceleration and try to keep below about 4,000 rpm for a petrol engine and 2,000 rpm for a diesel, for at least 1,000 miles. You should never work a cold engine hard, no matter how old it is, but should be especially careful not to do it with a new engine. It takes about four miles for an engine to reach its normal working temperature at which oil flows most freely, which is why many cars have water temperature gauges and high performance cars also have oil temperature gauges. A few cars, mostly Japanese and Korean, also have a blue or green warning light, showing a thermometer, which goes out when the engine reaches working temperature.

BRAKES

You should also avoid heavy use of the brakes because new brake pads also need to bed in as the friction materials wear to take account of any slight irregularities in the disc or drum.

TYRES

New tyres also need a couple of hundred miles to start giving their full grip so be particularly careful on new tyres in the wet. If you look at a tyre that has never been used you'll see why: manufacture leaves tiny spikes of rubber sticking up and keen edges to the tread blocks which need to be worn away before it can grip properly. New tyres may lose a little air in the first few days and wheel nuts should be checked for tightness after the first 30 miles (see Chapter 6).

Top tip

The run-in period for new brakes and tyres applies to old cars, too, and if the engine has had major work it is probably wise to go easy on it at first.

FEATHERED FIENDS

Finally, keep an eye on the paintwork because new paint is more vulnerable to damage from environmental contaminants like factory fallout and bird mess: seagull droppings are particularly damaging. You don't have to keep washing the car, just slosh the mess off.

10 THINGS TO REMEMBER

1 *Listen to what the salesperson tells you about the car at handover, noting anything needed to keep the warranty valid, like an early first service.*

2 *When you get the car home check it over for damage and problems.*

3 *Read the handbook.*

4 *Take time to get the correct driving position.*

5 *Seatbelts must always be adjusted to pass crash stress into your skeleton, not soft tissue.*

6 *Airbags are life savers but can cause injury if misused.*

7 *Use Isofix child seats if your car allows it and match them to the child's age and size.*

8 *Guard your keys and never leave them in an unattended car, even for a short time.*

9 *Make sure you know how to start your car correctly and whether it has any safety switches or immobilizers that might stop it starting.*

10 *Take it steady for the first few thousand miles and remember that new brakes and tyres need time to 'bed in'.*

5

....

Regular checks

In this chapter you will learn:
- **what needs checking and when**
- **how to reduce the risk of breakdowns**
- **essential car care equipment.**

In factories they have checklists that must be run through before a piece of machinery is started. Most would agree this is a sensible precaution to prevent damage to the machinery and injury to staff, yet few of us think of a car in the same way. But a car operates in a far more hostile environment than most factory machinery. It is subject to the often severe forces of speed, braking and cornering. It is battered by weather and debris from the road. Parts of it are asked to run at high temperatures while being doused in icy puddles. And while all this happens, you and your passengers, expect it to safely transport you hundreds of miles.

Walk around

Breakdown organizations say many call-outs could be avoided by the driver making simple visual checks on the car and its systems. For example, if, before you set out, you spot that one of your tyres is flatter than the others, then you'll avoid having to change a wheel on the motorway, yet most of us just get straight in and drive off.

The most basic check is what pilots call a walk around – a simple visual examination of the vehicle that can be done each time you return to it. It is especially wise if the car is parked on a street where it might be subject to vandalism or knocks from passing vehicles. You are looking for body damage, cracked lights, flat tyres, loose trim, foreign objects in or near tyres and even the neighbour's cat laying on a wheel.

It also pays to check things as you drive. Look for warning lights, listen for odd noises, be aware of how the car feels and be observant. The noise of an indicator clicker going faster than normal suggests a bulb has gone. The car pulling to one side on the way home when it was fine on the way to work could indicate a slow puncture and the reflection of your lights in other vehicles or shop windows can show you if they are all working.

Insight

One of the silliest things a car owner can do is ignore the thought 'I've never noticed that before'. OK, it might be a trick of the light on the bonnet or noise from an odd bit of road surface, but it could equally be a failed bonnet catch or a flat rear tyre. When it is safe to do so, pull over and check whatever you have noticed because a few minutes doing that could save a lot of grief and a much longer delay. I once failed to do this and drove on thinking the car didn't feel quite right, only to find that I must have been driving for some time with a punctured rear tyre which was then too badly damaged to repair.

Check session

But you must also have a regular check session when you give everything proper attention and top up anything that needs it. Your handbook explains where everything is and what the various identification and warning symbols around the engine mean. (See Plate 6.)

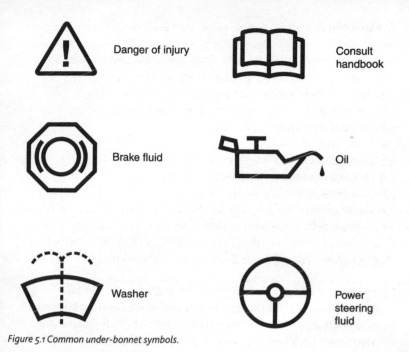

Figure 5.1 Common under-bonnet symbols.

HOW OFTEN?

The advice with modern cars is that a once a month check is usually enough. However, if you do more than 1,000 miles a month or have an older car, you should do it more often. Also if you have driven or are about to drive in adverse conditions, plan to carry a heavier than normal load or to go on a long journey, then a special round of checks is worthwhile.

When you get a new car, make the checks about once every two weeks for the first couple of months to get to know the quirks of the car. With your old car you knew it never needed oil between services and a washer bottle fill up normally lasted a month, but you do not know that with your new one. Also, brand new cars often need to settle in, so the tyres may lose pressure a little quicker than normal and the engine may use a little more oil as components bed in.

EQUIPMENT

You do not need anything high tech. You need the following:

▶ *tyre pressure gauge*
▶ *air pump*
▶ *tread depth gauge*
▶ *washer fluid*
▶ *combined window scraper and squeegee*
▶ WD40 *or similar lubricant spray*
▶ *kitchen towel*
▶ *hand cleaner*
▶ *latex gloves for sensitive skin.*

TYRE EQUIPMENT

A tyre pressure gauge is essential. Cheap ones can be a false economy, soon becoming inaccurate, and if your car has a space saver spare wheel on which the tyre pressure is high, a cheap gauge may not read high enough. Digital ones are easier to use but make sure they can be switched between imperial pounds per square inch (psi) and metric **bar** because some car handbooks only give one measurement. An electric air pump that plugs into a cigarette lighter socket is a lot easier than a foot pump and means you do not have to traipse off to the garage to use an air line for a few psi. A tyre tread depth gauge is better than guessing whether you have enough tread, though you don't need to use it every month. (See Plate 7.)

Insight

Do not trust pressure gauges that are built into air pumps. I have never known one to be accurate enough and some air is always lost as you disconnect the pump's airline from the valve. Built-in gauges are useful only in that they let you see if you have put in enough air to make it worth disconnecting the pump and checking with a separate gauge.

GLASS

Invest in windscreen washer fluid. Plain water will not cut through greasy road grime, tends to smear and freezes more easily. Washing up liquid foams up too much and is often high in salt, which is bad for the bodywork. Similarly, never use coolant **anti-freeze** in the washer bottle because it damages the wipers and paintwork.

Washer fluid is cheaper to buy as concentrate in five-litre containers and it is easier to use if you have a separate container in which to mix the correct amounts ready for use – that also saves time when you realize the washer bottle has run out just as you're off to work.

A window scraper with a foam piece on one side and squeegee on the other makes cleaning the windows easier.

LUBRICATION

A can of WD40 or similar spray lubricant is also a car owner's essential. It stops door hinges graunching, prevents locks icing, protects electrical contacts from corrosion and can repel water from ignition cables.

CLEANING UP

You'll need a few sheets of kitchen towel for wiping **dipsticks** and cleaning things off. If you have sensitive skin it may be sensible to wear thin latex gloves because many fluids in cars, including engine oil, trigger allergic reactions. Get some hand cleaner formulated for grease and oil because ordinary soap or household detergents can't remove it completely.

Insight

I use hand cleaners derived from vegetable products which are kinder to the skin and the environment than chemical-based cleaners.

Checklist

Here's what to check:

- ▶ *tyres*
- ▶ *oil*
- ▶ *coolant*
- ▶ *brake and other fluids*
- ▶ *washer bottle*
- ▶ *lights*
- ▶ *battery.*

Tyres

We'll be covering tyres in more detail in the next chapter but they are a vital part of your monthly check because they are all that keeps you on the road. Spotting problems early may not just save you from a puncture, it could prevent an accident or avoid your having to prematurely replace a tyre. Over- and under-inflation increase tyre-wear and affect handling while the latter increases fuel consumption and the risk of a **blow-out** through overheating.

PRESSURES

The most important thing is to check the tyre pressures, including the spare. The correct pressures are either on a sticker, usually inside a door frame or fuel filler flap, or in the handbook. If it is in the book, mark the page and mark the correct pressure for your car. The handbook is likely to list different pressures for different versions of the car and all the sizes of tyre fitted. It may also list higher pressures for full loads, high speed driving and trailer towing and should define what is meant by these things. For example, high speed may only mean autobahn driving with no speed limit for long periods.

Also, if the sun warms up one side of a parked car it creates higher pressure readings on that side, so it is best to do it in the shade or on cloudy days. Remember to replace the tyre valve dust caps because they stop dirt getting into the valve, which might make it stick open.

Top tip

Checking pressures is best done with the tyres cold because the pressure increases as the tyres warm up with use. If you do not have an air pump, take the pressures before setting off for a garage and then add the amount needed to whatever the warm pressure is. So if they were 3 psi low at home, add that amount to the higher warm tyre pressure. Take your pressure gauge with you because garage airline ones are often abused and not always accurate.

SOFT OPTIONS

Be wary of a tyre with pressure substantially down on the others. It may have a slow puncture which could become a fast one if you drive on it. Look for objects stuck in it and, if you can't find any, check the valve is not leaking by smearing saliva across the top and seeing if it forms a bubble. Chapter 6 of this book explains how to replace a valve core. If you are not going anywhere in the car you can reinflate the tyre and check it again later but if you plan a journey, especially using high speed roads, it is safer to put the spare on and have the tyre professionally examined.

CONDITION

While you are checking pressures, also give the tyres a visual once over. Look for cuts, bulges, uneven tyre-wear, low tread depth (all explained in the tyre chapter) and objects stuck in the tyre. It pays to run your hand over the inside wall of the tyre.

Oil

Oil is the blood of the engine. It lubricates and helps cool the engine as it is pumped from the sump at the bottom of the engine, through channels running around it like veins to the moving parts that need lubrication. Running low results in serious and expensive damage.

Some cars have oil level indicators that come on with the ignition, usually with a message like 'Oil OK'. These only work correctly on level ground and should not be seen as a complete alternative to a visual check.

DIPSTICK

Your handbook says where the oil dipstick is and whether the oil level should be checked with the engine hot or cold. It may also tell you how long you should let an engine that has been running stand to allow oil to drain back into the sump. It also says what the markers on the stick mean and, usually, how much oil is needed to raise the level from minimum to maximum.

Pull the dipstick out, taking care because long ones can flip drops of oil around as they come out. Wipe it with kitchen towel and put it all the way back in. Remove it again and check where the oil comes to. With new oil it can be difficult to see where it is on the dipstick but older oil is darker so the level can be easily seen. When doing this, also look out for signs of contamination. If the oil has deposits like mayonnaise on the dipstick or around the filler cap on

Figure 5.2 The handbook should say how much oil is needed to raise the level from min to max on the dipstick.

top of the engine, it means water is getting from the cooling system into the oil, probably because a gasket has failed. This needs professional attention quickly or serious damage could result.

Make sure you replace the dipstick and push it fully home (it usually clicks) because when the engine is running the oil is under pressure and may spray out if the dipstick isn't replaced properly. For the same reason, never remove it when the engine is running.

TOP UP

New cars rarely need more oil between services once they are run in, but old cars may constantly use a little oil and need topping up, especially if a service is nearly due. But if the oil level suddenly starts dropping faster than normal, the engine should be investigated by a mechanic because it is a sign of leaks or engine-wear (the latter is usually accompanied by exhaust smoke).

If you have to add oil, read the handbook for the specification you need. The oil's viscosity is described with a figure like 10W/40 which signifies its thickness at winter and summer temperatures. In addition, the handbook will say it must comply with minimum standards, usually giving an **SAE (Society of Automotive Engineers)** number, which is given somewhere on the oil can, and may say if the engine requires a synthetic oil or one specifically for diesels. Diesels are hard on their oil, require different additives to petrol engines and often need synthetic oils to achieve service intervals as long as petrol engines' intervals.

Oil is put into the engine through a filler located on top of it. Most have an oil symbol on them, like a dripping oil can. Let the engine cool before adding fresh oil and, even then, remember that what drips off the filler cap may be hot. Oil is usually sold in containers with necks shaped to make filling easy, but if you have problems, use a funnel or the top cut off a plastic bottle. Keep a rag handy to mop up spills or they smoke and smell when the engine gets hot.

Top tip

Do not overfill the engine because that can do as serious damage as having too little oil. It can even wreck the expensive catalytic converter that cleans exhaust fumes. Even if the handbook says how much oil you need, pause every so often to allow the oil to drain down and check the level with the dipstick, after wiping it off each time.

Fluid levels

Translucent plastics have made checking the levels of various fluids in cars much easier and safer. On all but the oldest cars you should be able to check most by just looking at the reservoir bottle so there is no risk of inadvertently introducing contaminants or undoing something where the contents are under pressure. However, make sure you identify the correct reservoir: you don't want to top up the brake system with washer fluid or vice versa. If levels drop substantially between services in these items they should be professionally checked.

COOLANT

The most obvious reservoir is usually the expansion tank for the cooling system (see Plate 8). Since the 1970s cars have been built with sealed cooling systems, where instead of venting to the air they have a large container into which coolant can pass when it heats up and expands, then be drawn from as it cools. These days the tank is made of clear plastic with levels marked for minimum and maximum, sometimes both hot and cold. Never remove the cap from the tank or the radiator when the engine is hot or you may be scalded by the escaping steam and coolant, which can be hotter than boiling water.

The coolant is a mixture of water and anti-freeze, which does much more than stop it freezing. It contains additives to stop sludge forming, prevent corrosion, to stop different metals reacting with each other and to raise the boiling point. If it needs topping up a little, you can use plain water but it is best to use an anti-freeze mixture, though check the handbook for the type of anti-freeze required (see box below).

Coolant shouldn't need much topping up and if it does, you should investigate the cause. First, check that the soft plastic or rubber washer in the expansion tank cap is clean and in good condition and if your car has a radiator cap, check that too. Next look for leaks: you may see dripping coolant but it is more likely you'll see the telltale white marks where coolant that has leaked under pressure has dried. Also look for mayonnaise deposits in the oil, as explained in the section above on oil.

If you can find no leaks, or have doubts about the condition of the expansion tank or radiator caps, buy a new cap but make sure you get the right one for your car. These caps are cheap so it is worth seeing if this fixes a minor drop in levels before you seek professional help, though if it doesn't solve the problem remember to tell the garage you have replaced it so they don't renew it. If the level keeps dropping, or drops fast, you'll have to get it professionally checked. A garage technician not only knows what to look for but has the facilities to be able to see all over the engine. Repairing a leaking system, even if you need a new radiator, is much cheaper than fixing an overheated engine.

Anti-freeze explained

Like so much else, anti-freeze is not as simple as it once was. Traditional anti-freeze, which required replacing every two years
(Contd)

or 30,000 miles, was called **inorganic acid technology (IAT)** but new formulae were developed to extend its life to five years or 150,000 miles. **Organic acid technology (OAT)** was introduced in the 1990s followed by **hybrid organic acid technology (HOAT)**, which is a mixture of IAT and OAT. There's also a nitrate organic acid technology anti-freeze but at the time of writing no car manufacturer used it. You don't need to know the technology behind this, just that mixing them isn't recommended because it shortens the life of the coolant and reduces its protective qualities. So just see what set of initials are applied to your car's anti-freeze in the handbook and what percentage of anti-freeze solution to water is required. It is best to mix anti-freeze with deionized water, though some stores stock ready mixed anti-freeze for topping up.

BRAKE FLUID

The next most important level to check is brake fluid. The reservoir for this is often attached to a large drum-shaped object, which is the brake servo for boosting the action of your push on the pedal. Some modern cars have pumped systems to do the job of the servo, but whatever you have, the reservoir is mounted on something from which many metal pipes run.

Again, the reservoir has maximum and minimum markings but any sudden drop in fluid levels is best investigated by experts. If brake fluid is leaking it may be contaminating the brake pads, reducing their stopping ability, and if that happens inside **drum brakes** (as opposed to **disc brakes**) it can be difficult to spot. This can be very dangerous because it can leave you with one brake not working, making the car slew to one side on heavy braking.

If you have to top up the fluid to get to a garage, thoroughly clean around the reservoir cap before undoing it and only use a freshly opened bottle of fluid that meets the specification given in the handbook, then make sure you replace the reservoir's cap tightly. These precautions are necessary because brake fluid absorbs water which, when the brakes get hot, creates water vapour bubbles in the system leading to brake fade. The fluid also needs replacing at mileages recommended by the manufacturer for the same reason. Brake fluid can damage paintwork.

Cars with hydraulic clutches may have a second reservoir like the brake fluid one and drops in levels should be treated in the same way as brake fluid for the same reason: out of sight, it could be contaminating the clutch plate.

STEERING

There may also be a translucent reservoir for the power steering, though it may have a metal or opaque plastic one with a dipstick inside the lid. If you have to take the lid off, clean around it first and make sure it is on tight afterwards.

TRANSMISSION

Some cars, notably automatics, also have a dipstick for the transmission oil, which is checked in the same way as engine oil.

WASHERS

The thing you most often have to top up is the washer bottle. It is a legal requirement to have working windscreen washers as well as being common sense. As we said earlier, it is easiest to have a container of washer fluid made up. Some washer bottles have a mesh insert in the neck to stop debris getting in and blocking the washer jets and others have a mesh guard on the outlet pipe. If you have to use rainwater to fill the washer, filter it through a piece of cloth because once debris gets into the washer pipes it is very difficult to remove.

Electrics

BATTERIES

Batteries are often 'maintenance free', but that doesn't mean they can be ignored. Flat batteries are the most common reason for breakdown organizations to be called out, though this is often down to driver errors, like leaving the lights on.

Even with a maintenance-free battery you should still check the connections are tight and the bracket holding it in place is sound. Also look for the furry residue left by leaking electrolyte which suggests the casing is damaged and the battery should be replaced.

With batteries that are not maintenance free you must check the level of electrolyte. Some have translucent sides with minimum and maximum level markings to make this easy but if it hasn't, you remove the filler plug or plugs and shine a thin beamed torch in. The electrolyte should cover the metal battery plates inside by about a centimetre and if it doesn't it should be topped up with distilled or deionized water, but do not overfill it. This is easier if you use a container with a thin plastic hose attached.

Batteries are covered in more detail in Chapter 7.

LIGHTS

Don't forget to check the lights for damage and failed bulbs. You must turn on the ignition to get all the lights to work. If a headlight works on beam but not dip, or vice versa, it usually means the bulb has failed, but if it works on neither it is likely to be a wiring problem because it is unusual for both filaments to go at the same time. In some cars the rear lights also have double filaments with the second coming on as a brake light, but most cars now have separate brake lights.

If you haven't got a helper, you may be able to check brake lights by the reflections in a vehicle behind or against your garage door. Remember, if one brake light bulb has failed the chances are the other will go soon, leaving drivers behind with no warning you are stopping.

Indicators flash quicker if a bulb on that side has failed, though don't rely on this because a failed **side repeater indicator**, and some high tech electronic systems, may not produce this effect.

....
Top tip
Check indicators individually, not by using the hazard warning light switch, which is usually a different circuit. If there is a wiring fault on the indicators it might not be revealed by the hazard lights.
....

Many modern cars have **light emitting diodes** (**LED**) instead of bulbs in side and brake lights and indicators. Most high level brake lights (the one in the centre at the back) and modern daylight driving lights are LED. These do not have a filament to burn out so they should last the life of the car, but this also means that if they don't work, you probably have a wiring problem that needs checking.

Can you see?

Dirty windows and mirrors increase the risk of you missing something important and make long journeys more tiring as your eye and brain try to cope with the interference to your vision, especially at night. Dirt on the inside also makes demisting take longer.

OUTSIDE

Don't use household window cleaning preparations on the outside of car windows, because they often contain silicones which make the water bead up and stop the wipers clearing it effectively. Either use glass cleaners prepared for cars, washing up liquid or windscreen washer solution.

> **Top tip**
> If you can't get rid of oily smearing on the glass, use undiluted washer fluid, washing up liquid or methylated spirits, followed by normal cleaning, but don't forget to clean the wiper blades.

Splattered insects can be difficult to get off glass. There are special preparations that unstick them, but wear gloves because they dry out your skin. Much easier is to soak the splatters, then either use a car washing brush or get a 'bug sponge' from a car accessory shop. This is a sponge with a stiff foam on one side which is not as abrasive as a pot scouring sponge (some of which mark glass) but is stiffer than the body scrub sponges sold for washing people.

> **Insight**
> In summer I carry a damp bug sponge in a Ziploc plastic bag to debug the windscreen.

INSIDE

You can use the chalky liquid household glass cleaners (like Windowlene) inside the car, though those specially formulated for cars do a better, and often easier, job because they can handle the mist-like fallout on car windows. This mist is called plasticizer migration and is where a chemical used in manufacturing plastics leaches out of the car's trim and condenses on the glass, which is why it tends to be worse in new cars and in the summer. If this is really bad and your glass cleaner can't shift it, try wiping the glass with methylated or white spirit first, though make sure you have plenty of ventilation.

Take care if wearing rings when cleaning heated rear screens as they can scratch the heating element.

Smooth operating

While you are going round the car, check the operation of doors, locks and latches. Some modern cars have lubrication-free hinges with plastic inserts but if a door hinge squeals when you open it or is stiff, give it a squirt of WD40. Not only is it more pleasant to live with quiet doors but the screeching means metal is rubbing against metal creating wear that lubrication will stop.

Be careful about oiling door latches, though, because of the risk of getting oil on your clothes as you get in and out of the car. Most are designed not to need it.

A squirt of WD40 into door locks makes the key operate more smoothly and helps prevent them freezing.

Bonnet catches are usually greased as part of a service, though squirting lubricant down the release cable's sheath can help stop it sticking.

10 THINGS TO REMEMBER

1   *Get into the habit of walking round the car before driving off.*

2   *At least once a month check tyres, oil, coolant, fluids, washer bottle, lights and battery.*

3   *Check tyre pressures when cold, if possible.*

4   *If you need to top up oil or coolant check the specification in the handbook.*

5   *Low levels of any fluid are a warning that systems may be leaking.*

6   *Never remove a coolant reservoir or radiator cap from a hot engine or you risk scalding.*

7   *Take care when checking or working around batteries and remove jewellery first.*

8   *Keep lights clean and check them for damage and failed bulbs.*

9   *Keep windows clean but avoid using household glass cleaners on the windscreen where they may stop the wipers clearing efficiently.*

10 *If door hinges and catches do not work smoothly and quietly don't ignore it, lubricate them.*

6

....

Tyres

In this chapter you will learn:
- *legal and technical requirements*
- *how to spot faults*
- *how to buy new tyres.*

No matter how sophisticated your car is, the tyres are all that keeps
it on the road. The contact area for each tyre is about the same
as the sole of a man's foot and in the wet the tread has to move
thousands of litres of water a minute to be able to grip the tarmac.
To ensure maximum tread contact when cornering and hitting
bumps, the tyre walls must be flexible, but they must also be strong
enough to take the weight of the car and stresses of cornering.
In addition, think of the heat generated by friction and flexing as
it does all this at high speeds – a tyre on a high performance car
driven hard on a track is often too hot to touch.

If a tyre was the simple lump of rubber many motorists believe, it
would not be able to do its job and last for many miles. In fact, the
tread alone may contain three different rubber compounds with a
hard-wearing outer layer, a softer but durable underlay reinforced
with three layers of steel with other materials, like **Kevlar** which is
used in bullet-proof vests, and then a supple inner layer that must be
airtight. The side walls are reinforced with layers of polyester, rayon
or Kevlar, or a mixture of those. The **bead**, which is the edge round
the opening, contains a steel cable set in a special rubber compound
to seal the tyre onto the rim. These different structures are put

together in a mould and cooked under steam and pressure to bond all the components together. Misusing a tyre, perhaps by running it under-inflated, can create enough heat to undo this process resulting in the tyre 'delaminating' and the layers breaking up.

Writing on the wall

Once you realize how complex tyres are, you realize why there is so much information moulded into the tyre sidewall. Some of it is highly technical and may refer to legal requirements in other countries but we'll explain the more important ones because they are referred to later in the chapter.

SIZE

The biggest lettering, after the maker's name, is the basic tyre size and specification information. On a modest car it might read something like:

175/60 R 13 77 H

- ▶ *The 175 is the tyre's cross section, or tread width, measurement in millimetres.*
- ▶ *The 60 is its aspect ratio (sometimes called the profile) which is the height of the sidewall as a percentage of the tyre width, with 60 being a pretty average tyre these days.*
- ▶ *The letter R shows that this is a radial tyre: a crossply says C. Radial and crossply refers to the way the reinforcing layers are arranged in the tyre and radials are more flexible, giving better grip than crossplies, which are rarely used on cars today.*
- ▶ *The figure 13 is the wheel diameter in inches and a lower-profile tyre would need a bigger wheel – perhaps as much as 18 or 19 inches diameter.*
- ▶ *The 77 H refers to the tyre's load and speed rating (see the 'Weight and speed' section below).*

Ride vs handling

Some very high performance cars have a tyre aspect ratio of 50 or less resulting in a wide tyre with a sidewall so short it may look like a flat tyre.

These low-profile tyres flex less under cornering so, up to a point, improve handling but ride deteriorates, with much more small bump reaction coming through to the occupants, and road noise may increase significantly. So, think twice before opting for larger wheels and lower-profile tyres than are necessary for your car – the slight improvement in handling may not be worth the drawbacks.

It is a sad fact that for some years marketing people have had a strong influence on what wheels and tyres cars have fitted as standard. They feel it is important for cars to look 'young' and sporty so they are often fitted with lower profile tyres than are necessary. Bizarrely, that means you often find the cheaper models in the range, which are fitted with smaller wheels carrying taller profile tyres, have better ride than the more luxurious models with larger, smarter wheels and lower profile tyres.

WEIGHT AND SPEED

On the tyre in the example above, the code 77 H shows it is rated at 412 kg and up to 130 mph, so it would be fine on a small, low powered hatchback but would not be suitable for a heavy trailer or 140 mph sports version of the same hatchback. When you buy a tyre you would only quote the weight rating if it was for a heavy trailer or van. You would only quote the speed rating if it was for a modified car because if you say you want a tyre of a certain size for a certain model, the dealer will be able to see what rating it should be in his listings. These ratings are always higher than the car needs because they must have some leeway for safety. For example, if you multiply 412 by four it suggests the tyre is suitable for something weighing 1,648 kg, which is quite a big car, but manufacturers have to take account of uneven weight distribution, especially if carrying lots of luggage, and of people overloading their cars.

OTHER DATA

In areas subject to prolonged cold weather, dealers also sell winter tyres which are made of a rubber compound formulated for use in temperatures constantly below 7°C and have tread optimized for rain, snow and ice. Winter tyres have a lower speed rating than normal tyres of the same size and may overheat if run at speed on dry roads, which is why they are rarely used where winters are mild, like most of the UK.

Other data on the tyre include a manufacturing date as the month and year number, like 129 for December 2009, and DOT Codes and E marks which show it complies with the American Department of Transport and European Union requirements.

Somewhere on the tyre there will be a maximum pressure marked in psi and/or bar. This is not a running pressure – that's in your handbook – but a maximum that must not be exceeded, for example, when reinflating a repaired tyre.

Legal requirements

Tyres on the same axle must be of similar construction, so you can't use a radial tyre on one side and a crossply on the other. This is a legal requirement in most countries and good advice everywhere. In spite of this you are allowed to use a space saver spare wheel – a narrower tyre with a different construction to a standard tyre – as long as you stick to the manufacturer's speed limit, which may be given in kph (see your handbook and a sticker on the wheel).

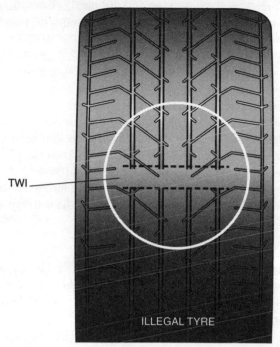

TWI

ILLEGAL TYRE

Figure 6.1 The tyre tread-wear indicator shows as a bar when the tread is below the legal limit.

In the UK, car tyres must have a legal minimum of 1.6 mm of tread across the central 75 per cent of the tread width for the whole circumference of the tyre. All tyres have tread-wear indicators whose position is shown by tiny arrows or trade marks on the tread edge. When the tyre reaches the legal minimum this shows as a bar across the tread, but by the time it appears the tread is virtually illegal and offering little grip, so use a tyre tread depth gauge to check it. Tyres with less than 4 mm of tread can't move water quickly enough, greatly increasing the risk of aquaplaning – where a cushion of water forms under the tyre, lifting it from the road.

It is also illegal to use a tyre with cuts deep enough to show the reinforcing layers. That is because of the risk of the tyre rupturing under stress, which could mean loss of control at speed or when cornering.

In the UK, tyres can't project beyond the car's bodywork, so if you fit exceptionally wide tyres you may need wheel-arch extensions too.

Insight

I can't remember the last time I replaced a tyre for worn out tread alone. When the tread gets thin, the tyre becomes much more prone to damage from objects cutting or puncturing it. This is especially so in rural areas where more damaging debris, like sharp stones, gets washed onto roads. Sometimes you will have to replace the tyre early because a cut is too deep or a puncture is too big to repair, but there is also little point paying for a puncture repair on a tyre you will soon have to replace.

Pressures

The car and tyre manufacturers work together to establish the best tyre pressures for your car. The handbook may give several sets of pressures for different sizes of tyre fitted to various models in the range. This is because the pressures required to carry the car's weight and cope with its performance vary according to the flexibility of the tyre.

In addition, while some cars only have one set of pressures, others' handbooks give different pressures for normal and full loads and high speeds. Most handbooks define what they mean by these things. For example, a normal load might be up to four people with no luggage while a full load is five people and luggage. High speed generally refers to driving at speeds in excess of 80 mph for long periods.

PRESSURES AND EFFICIENCY

We covered checking pressures in the previous chapter and they are important because this complex component of the car can only work properly if they are correct. If tyres are under-inflated they flex too much, which at speed creates heat with the danger of the tyre breaking up. It may allow an upward curve in the tyre's tread so the centre of the tread has less contact with the ground than it should. Together, heat and uneven tread pressure increase wear while the increased flexing of the tyre also increases its rolling resistance so it needs more of a push to rotate, which increases fuel consumption. So, apart from the safety aspect, under-inflated tyres increase running costs.

Don't be tempted to over-inflate car tyres to try to cut fuel bills because that too can increase tyre-wear by forcing an outward curve on the tread resulting in more wear on the centre. It also reduces grip by not allowing the tyre to flex enough to cope with bumps and cornering and by creating that curve on the tread. It can also seriously affect handling in other ways because the suspension is set up to work with the tyres at certain pressures. By over-inflating them you change the way it responds. Your steering might then feel over light and the car's cornering attitude changes.

EQUALITY

Remember, too, that four-wheel drive systems that distribute drive according to grip, and most electronic driving aids, work by comparing wheel rotation speeds. Over- or under-inflation increases or reduces the tyre's circumference so it rotates at a different speed to a correctly inflated tyre. Incorrect pressures can affect the efficiency of these systems, especially if it is only on one wheel.

Uneven tyre pressures also often make themselves felt by the car behaving differently when it corners to the left and right. The difference may be slight, but in cars with good road feel an attentive driver will notice it and should check the pressures.

CORE ISSUES

If you find a tyre on which the pressure has dropped, check the valve is not stuck or faulty. If you wipe saliva across the open end of the valve it will form a bubble if the valve is leaking. Inside the valve is a valve core, which is a tiny metal and plastic device that is held shut by air pressure and opened when a central pin is pushed down by an airline nozzle or other object. The sides of the core are threaded so it screws into the valve tube, which is also threaded. Sometimes dirt gets in and jams it partially open or the core just works loose and needs tightening. You can buy packets of them in car accessory shops and need a special tool to tighten or replace them, though some tyre pressure gauges include one. It's a metal or plastic rod with a slot across the end and a hole in the middle: the slot grips the core's shoulder and the hole is for the valve's pin.

Take care when undoing the valve because the sudden release of pressure can fire debris, including the valve core and tool, into your face. When you have replaced the valve core you must completely reinflate the tyre so you need access to either a garage airline or a powered pump.

Tyre faults

When you check tyres you must also look for damage and wear. As explained earlier, deep cuts, showing the reinforcing, mean immediate replacement is essential, as does any sign of the tyre breaking up, like missing bits of tread.

A less obvious danger is a lump or distortion in the tyre sidewall. This means air is getting between the layers of the tyre, so it is breaking up on the inside, which could result in a blow-out at speed, where the tyre suddenly disintegrates. It must be replaced.

It may sound obvious, but anything sticking in a tyre should be removed. A pointed stone or a small screw may not be long enough to puncture the tyre in one go, but it could work its way in if you carry on driving. In addition, you don't know it is a short screw until you pull it out. It is possible for a long object to pierce the tyre and not produce immediate deflation, but it could cause a sudden collapse at speed.

Uneven tread wear can reveal a number of problems if you know how to read it and, if spotted early enough, could save the cost of having to prematurely replace a tyre.

If the tyre has patches where the tread is more worn it suggests the wheel is not balanced properly. If the wheel is unbalanced, especially on the front, you usually feel a vibration at certain speeds. Any tyre dealer can balance the wheel and it only costs a few pounds. Balancing involves a machine that shows where the wheel and tyre have a heavier spot, through manufacture or wear, so a small weight can be attached to the rim to counter its effect. Without it, the wheel does not rotate at an even speed because the heavy spot always wants to get to the bottom faster than the lighter side, which causes the vibration you feel.

If the tread is worn up both edges, this suggests under-inflation because the tread has curved inwards in the middle, increasing wear at the edges, but if the increased wear is up the centre of the tread it suggests over-inflation because the centre is being pushed out. If you get either of these problems when you have regularly checked the pressures, make sure you are using the right ones and that your pressure gauge is accurate.

Top tip

Ask a tyre dealer to compare your pressure gauge with theirs, which are usually calibrated.

Tread wear up one side of the tyre, often accompanied by feathering along one edge of the tread blocks, suggests the wheels are out of alignment. If this is bad, you may also notice the car pulling to one side. The suspension and steering are set up to present the wheels to the road at a precise angle and hitting something hard, like a deep pothole or kerb, can misalign the wheels. The wheel is then going along at the wrong angle, scrubbing off tread as it does so. If tyres show the slightest sign of this sort of wear, get alignment (sometimes called tracking) checked. Many tyre dealers do it free

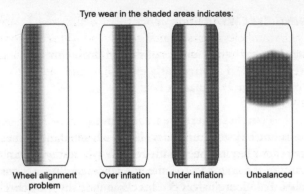

Tyre wear in the shaded areas indicates:

Wheel alignment problem   Over inflation   Under inflation   Unbalanced

Figure 6.2 Uneven tyre wear (shaded areas) reveals potential problems.

and only charge if adjustment is needed, which costs less than replacing a tyre. However, if the tread has worn too much up one side you may have to replace the tyre anyway because the car will never run true on a tyre with a wedge-shaped cross section, which might also increase wear on other tyres.

Repairs and replacements

Repairs must be done by qualified technicians. Unfortunately, not all punctures are repairable, which may mean scrapping a nearly new tyre, but your safety is at stake.

UNREPAIRABLE DAMAGE

Punctures in the sidewall, or close to it, can't be repaired and neither can large holes, like where a large stone has gone through. The maximum number of repairs allowed in a tyre is three. In cases where carrying out a repair would result in the tyre being unsafe, some dealers will do it if you are stupid enough to demand it and sign a disclaimer agreeing you have been told. Where the repair would be illegal, they must refuse to do it.

Some people get round this situation by fitting an inner tube, but this is not possible on all wheels and is a false economy because it doesn't last long. In addition, inner tubes deflate much more suddenly than tubeless tyres, which could lead to loss of control and is why it is extremely dangerous on trailers, caravans and high performance cars.

BALANCING

When a puncture is repaired the wheel needs rebalancing because the weight of a plug has been added to the tyre and you can't be sure of getting the tyre back on the wheel in exactly the same place as before. Most dealers do this automatically, but check it is done.

PRICING REPLACEMENTS

If you know you're going to have to replace a tyre it is a good idea to phone round for prices. If you have to replace one unexpectedly, because of an unrepairable fault, you must decide whether to do it then and there and risk paying more or whether you want to drive round without a spare until you can find the best price – which could well be at the dealer you're currently in. If you're a long way from home, the former action is wiser.

Top tip
> Tyres are something where small local firms often at least match the big national companies and may even invite you to try the big boys first.

Make sure prices quoted include VAT, fitting, balancing and a new valve (it is usual and sensible to replace the valves when you renew tyres). Very cheap brands you've never heard of are often a false economy because they don't last as long as the big names but, equally, if you are offered two big names it is probably not worth paying for the dearer one. However, there is a lot to be said for staying with the car maker's original choice, if it is not too pricey, because you know it suits the car.

Before you phone round you need to make a note of the car's make, model and model year (or registration) and the size of the tyres fitted (like 175/70 R 13). The dealer will be able to look up tyres of that size with suitable weight and speed ratings.

TIME FOR CHANGE

If you are unhappy with the current tyre, perhaps because it is noisy on local road surfaces or keeps getting punctures, discuss this with local tyre dealers. They often know alternatives that work. For example, they may know that one brand copes better with rural life than another because its tread pattern is less likely to trap the flints that get washed onto roads in some areas. If you have special needs, like needing to do serious off-road work in difficult conditions, talk to your car manufacturer first because they may be able to suggest tested tyres to enable the car to do what you want.

Tread carefully

Having different tread patterns won't make much difference on most cars, though different tread depth can. On any car, having a new tyre on one side and a nearly worn out one on the other is unwise because one side has so much more grip than the other. It can also upset electronic driving aids because of the differences in wheel rotation speeds, and on driven axles, especially with four-wheel-drive systems, it can cause mechanical stress. So if you replace a tyre and the one on the other side is well worn, consider replacing that as well. If your spare is unused you could swap it for the partially worn tyre.

Top tip

If you replace a pair of tyres, put them on the back and put what were the backs on opposite sides at the front. This gives you greater grip at the back and extends the tyres' life by getting them worn in without having to steer the car.

Spares

Once, all cars had five wheels and tyres that were all the same, but other arrangements are increasingly common.

STEEL SPARES

A few cars with alloy wheels have a steel spare with the same size and type of tyre as the alloys. This is just a cost-cutting measure and rarely seen these days because it was unpopular with customers. This arrangement does not always require you to stick to a speed limit, but take care because you have one wheel a lot heavier than the others.

SPACE-SAVERS

Space-saver spares are increasingly popular because they save boot space, especially on cars with wide tyres. These always come with a speed limit for safe use, usually about 50 mph, which is given in the handbook and on a sticker on the wheel (they may say 80 kph so don't get confused). Space-saver wheels are brightly coloured so it is obvious to the police if you are ignoring the manufacturer's safety requirements. Space-savers usually require very high tyre pressures. (See Plate 9.)

Temporary repair kits

Some cars, usually high performance ones, have temporary repair equipment instead of a spare. The temporary repair equipment may be either a canister of compressed gas with a sealant, which seals the hole and inflates the tyre in one go or, more commonly, a sealant and an electric tyre pump. Read the handbook to find out how to use these and what speeds and mileage limits the repairs have. (See Plate 10.)

Insight

A friend of mine experienced the major problem with repair kits after a piece of metal made a finger-sized hole in her tyre, so no amount of sealant could mend it. Given the choice, I would go for a spare or runflat tyre (see below) over a repair kit.

Runflat

Runflat tyres do just what their name suggests. You can't run an ordinary tyre while it's flat for two reasons: there is little to hold it on the rim, and the squashed sidewalls will be damaged by the weight of the car on them. So, apart from being dangerous, it could write off a tyre that would have been repairable. Runflat tyres are designed to fit special rims so they won't roll off when deflated and have reinforced sidewalls with a lubricant to prevent friction as the collapsed edges of the wall rub together.

Most cars with runflat systems also have a puncture or low pressure warning symbol in the instruments. Read your handbook to find out what warning systems it has and what mileage and speed limits there are on a flat tyre.

ONE WAY

Some very high performance tyres have unidirectional treads which can only rotate in one direction. This is normally because the tread pattern is asymmetric so the outer edge has a different pattern to the inner one. If a car with this sort of tyre has a full-sized spare wheel it may carry a sticker saying which side it is intended for but if not, look for the direction of rotation arrows moulded into the side wall. If you have to fit it on the other side of the car, keep your speed down and get it changed quickly. The handbook may recommend a maximum speed.

Tyre rotation

Tyres wear at different rates according to what axle they are on and whether the car is front- or rear-wheel drive. The front tyres usually wear faster because they are turned to steer the car.

To counter this, some tyre and car manufacturers suggest rotating the tyres periodically. How often depends on who you talk to, with tyre makers suggesting anything from 2,000 to 6,000 miles and some car makers including it in the service schedule.

ROTATE OR NOT

There are also those who advise against it because it means
you have to replace four tyres at once instead of two at a time.
However, if your mileage is right, rotating tyres on a car you
bought new may mean never having to replace them because they'll
last your ownership. For example, if after 18 months the front
tyres have lost half their tread depth and the backs have lost a
quarter, swapping them means in 18 months' time they should
all still have a quarter of their tread.

HOW TO DO IT

Should you choose to do it, the way you rotate them depends on
which wheels are driven by the engine. On front-drive cars the
advice is to put the fronts on the same sides at the back while
putting what were the back wheels onto their opposite sides at the
front (left back to right front). On rear-drive and **4WD**, the backs
go to the same sides on the front and what were the front go to
opposite sides on the back.

To rotate wheels yourself, take one wheel off and replace it with
the spare, then work your way round the car, replacing the spare
last. If your car doesn't have a spare, ask the garage to do it as

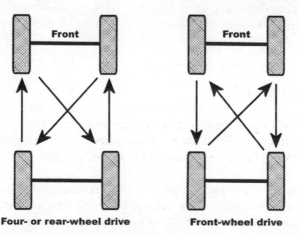

Four- or rear-wheel drive   Front-wheel drive

Figure 6.3 Tyre rotation varies according to which wheels are driven.

part of a service. You can't rotate the wheels on cars fitted with unidirectional tyres.

Note: Changing a wheel is covered under breakdowns in Chapter 10.

Running in

New tyres need running in to take off little pimples and spikes created during manufacture and to smooth off the edges of the tread. So take it steady for the first couple of hundred miles, avoiding hard acceleration, braking and cornering, and keeping a close eye on pressures.

Whenever a wheel has been removed you should check the tightness of the wheel nuts after about 30 miles, but don't use excessive force or you can damage the threads.

10 THINGS TO REMEMBER

1 *Tyres are all that keeps you on the road.*

2 *Incorrect tyre pressures reduce the tyre's grip, cause increased tyre wear and increase fuel consumption.*

3 *Replacement tyres must be the correct speed and weight rating for the car.*

4 *You must not mix radial and crossply tyres on the same axle.*

5 *If a tyre is losing air check the valve is not leaking.*

6 *Uneven tyre wear is an indication of a fault like unbalanced or misaligned wheels.*

7 *Punctures that are too large or close to the sidewall cannot be repaired.*

8 *The maximum number of repairs allowed on a tyre is three.*

9 *Replace tyres with bulges or cuts deep enough to show reinforcing.*

10 *Tyres significantly lose grip well before reaching the legal minimum of 1.6 mm of tread.*

7

Batteries

In this chapter you will learn:
* *how to look after batteries*
* *about battery faults*
* *how to replace batteries.*

Battery safety ⚠

We must stress again that batteries are dangerous. They are low voltage compared to household electricity but it is direct current, so if your body or tools make a connection between live and neutral terminals (which includes the car's bodywork) the current holds you instead of jolting you away as the alternating current in your house would. That is always painful and can cause deep burns, so remove watches and jewellery when working near the battery and, if possible, use insulated tools.

The electrolyte liquid in the battery is a very powerful acid capable of serious corrosive skin burns and should be washed off immediately. If it gets into the eyes, flush it out with lots of water and seek immediate medical help. If it is swallowed, do not induce vomiting but seek urgent medical attention.

Do not inspect batteries with a naked flame because they give off hydrogen which, when mixed with air, ignites explosively. This is especially likely when batteries are being recharged.

Because batteries contain lead they are very heavy so take care when lifting them and make sure they are properly secured in the car when in use or being transported.

Dispose of batteries responsibly by taking them to a recycling facility.

Battery problems are the most common reason for breakdown organizations to be called out. This is frequently down to human error, like leaving lights on, but often it is because of preventable faults due to poor maintenance, damage or simple old age.

Please note that we are talking about conventional petrol and diesel engined cars where the battery is primarily a starter battery. Electric powered cars and hybrid power cars use specialist batteries, usually lithium ion, and their use and maintenance is explained in the car's handbook.

We covered the basic regular checks on a battery in Chapter 5 and jump-starting is explained in Chapter 10 on breakdowns.

What does it do?

Modern cars use a lot of power even when parked, when the battery powers alarms, information storage systems and comfort items like stereos. A 1960s car consumed about 300 watts of power but even a modest modern one uses more than three times that – and that is without using the starter. The starter needs a terrific amount of power to turn the engine over, especially on a cold day, which is why failure to start is the most major problem resulting from poor battery condition.

A car battery stores power rather than producing it through chemical reaction like an alkaline battery in a torch. The battery is charged by the **alternator,** a type of generator driven by a belt from the engine. When you switch something on, with the car running, the power is drawn first from the alternator, but if that is unable to produce enough, perhaps because the car is at idle with lots of equipment turned on, power is drawn from the battery. As you drive off and engine speed increases, the alternator is able to produce enough power both to run the devices and charge the battery. That is why short journeys in poor weather can be such a drain on the battery.

Indeed, the battery manufacturer Varta suggests that cars used mainly for short journeys may benefit from having a battery of greater capacity than is usual for the car. This doesn't mean it produces more than 12 volts but that it can store more power.

When you start the car you are relying purely on stored power because the alternator can't produce more until the engine is running.

How does it work?

Inside the battery are sets of electrode plates welded together. The positive ones are lead dioxide and the negative ones are sponge lead while ions passing between them are carried by the sulphuric acid electrolyte. As the battery discharges (gives out electricity) lead sulphate is formed, but when it is recharged by the alternator that is turned back into lead dioxide and sulphuric acid.

Cars made since the 1960s have what is known as a negative earth. This means the negative terminal on the battery is connected to the car's body. This earths it and means that when components are connected up, the negative connection can be made to the nearest part of the body.

Giving it a hand

You can reduce the drain on your battery by switching off unnecessary items, which also reduces fuel consumption. Don't put miserliness before road safety, but every time the alternator has to work harder to supply more power, it adds to fuel consumption. Admittedly it isn't much – a rear wiper uses about 0.2 litres of petrol an hour – but it adds up.

BATTERY HELPING TIPS

▶ *As soon as a high drain device, like the heated rear screen, has done its job, switch it off.*
▶ *Avoid sitting in a parked car with everything turned on, even with the engine running.*
▶ *Don't turn things on until after you have started the car, leaving non-essentials like radios and phone chargers until ready to pull away.*
▶ *Push the clutch pedal down when starting. This will reduce the load on the starter.*
▶ *Turn off interior lights if you have the car doors open for long periods, like when cleaning it.*
▶ *Run the engine if you use appliances that plug into the cigarette lighter, like tyre pumps or car vacuum cleaners.*

Early warning

If the battery has trouble starting the car, don't ignore this early warning. It could suggest something simple, like a faulty connection, low electrolyte or the boot light staying on, which can be quickly rectified before you are left stranded.

If a battery fails to start the car more than once, get it professionally checked because you don't want to be stranded somewhere without even the power to run **hazard warning lights**.

Maintenance

Many batteries now are called maintenance free, which means they do not need topping up because they have sealed systems. However, even these need some care.

Check the connections to the terminals are tight and smear them with petroleum jelly (Vaseline) to prevent corrosion. Do not use other greases because many conduct electricity.

Keep the top of the battery clean because dirt traps moisture on damp days and allows power to 'leak' between the terminals. If you get white chemical deposits on the battery, the acid is leaking out. On a maintenance-free battery this can only mean the casing is cracked so the battery must be replaced. On batteries that aren't maintenance free it may only mean that one of the top-up plugs hasn't been put back properly and the deposits need to be washed off with water.

Batteries that are not maintenance free need the electrolyte levels checked. If it is low, top it up with distilled or deionized water to either the maximum filling mark on the outside of the battery or, if it doesn't have markings, to about 1 cm above the lead plates.

Plate 1 Some three-point rear centre seatbelts have two buckles, often colour coded.

Plate 2 This luxury car offers infinite electric seat adjustments with three memory buttons.

Plate 3 A correctly fitted seatbelt crossing the breastbone and hips.

Plate 4 Using a key to turn the screw-head style of child lock.

Plate 5 A fully automatic air conditioning system electronically controls temperature, distribution and fan boosting.

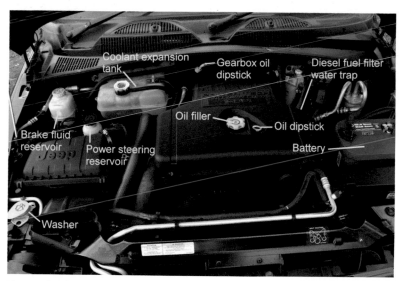

Plate 6 The things you need to check under a bonnet, though they are not this easy to see in all cars.

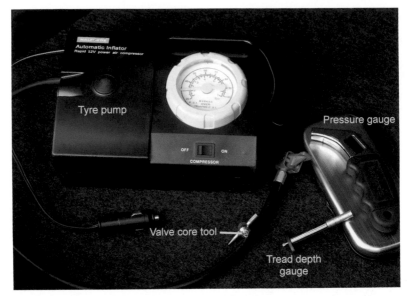

Plate 7 Tyre check equipment.

Plate 8 Translucent plastics make checking levels easy, but note the warning symbols on this coolant reservoir.

Plate 9 A space saver spare alongside a normal wheel, showing the difference in tyre size and the bright wheel colour.

Plate 10 Instead of a spare wheel, some cars have a temporary repair kit with a pump that blows air and puncture sealant fluid into the tyre.

Plate 11 A curry comb – used to remove pet hairs from carpets.

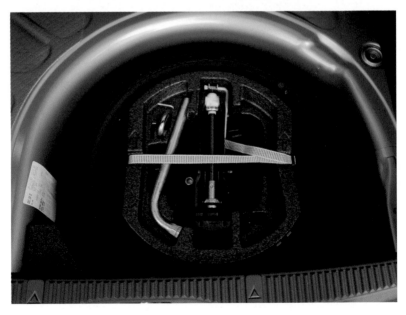

Plate 12 Tyre-changing tools must be correctly stowed for safety.

Plate 13 Motorway marker posts carry a unique location number and directions to the nearest emergency phone.

Plate 14 Car fuse boxes usually include a set of tweezers for removing fuses.

Buying batteries

All car batteries are 12 volt but there are other considerations including capacity, cold crank ability and lots of other extremely technical stuff. As explained earlier, capacity is the amount of electricity the battery can store and is usually shown in ampere hours (Ah). Cold crank or cold start capacity is how much power it can put out for how long at −18°C.

Simpler considerations when buying a battery are its physical size and what type of connections it has. There is no point buying a battery with round pole terminals if your car's battery leads are for flat ones.

If you tell the dealer the make, model and model year (or registration number) of your car they can look up what you need to fit. In some cases you may need to give a Vehicle Identification Number (VIN) if the battery requirements changed close to when your car was registered. Battery manufacturers also have vehicle-to-battery matching facilities on their websites and the car's handbook should give the specifications.

However, if you have modified the car, perhaps by putting in a massively powerful stereo system, or regularly make short journeys and have trouble starting, you might want to discuss fitting a battery with greater capacity.

Top tip

Batteries are items well worth phoning round for prices on. If you do, don't forget your car make's franchised dealer because they can sometimes match fast fit outlets while supplying the manufacturer's original equipment battery. Beware of false economies, too, because it is worth paying extra for maintenance-free batteries and long warranties.

Right connections

If you replace the battery yourself, check which battery cable goes directly to the car's body – this is the earth lead. On very old cars it may be the positive (red) lead but on cars made since the 1960s it is usually the negative (black) lead and all modern cars have a negative earth. Disconnect the earth lead first then disconnect the other (live) lead. This means if you touch part of the car's body with your tools or hands while disconnecting the live terminal you will not short circuit yourself.

Put the replacement battery in place and make sure it is properly bolted down using the proper fixings. If they are damaged, replace them because you don't want something as heavy as a battery flying around or falling over and leaking acid or making contact with metalwork. When reconnecting a battery, connect the live lead first, then the earth lead to avoid zapping yourself.

Responsible disposal ⚠

If a dealer replaces the battery for you, they will dispose of the old one. If you replace the battery yourself, make sure the old one is kept out of reach of children until you can take it to your local household refuse site or recycling centre. Your council can tell you which sites can accept them. Dispose of them properly because they can cause serious environmental damage as well as serious injury to anyone or anything coming in contact with them, while the lead in them can be recycled.

Charging

If your battery is flat at home, you may want to charge it from the mains. Only use a charger designed specifically for car batteries or you risk fire, injury and damage to the battery or charger.

CHOOSING CHARGERS

The best chargers automatically regulate the power going to the battery as it charges, easing back on it as it nears full charge and cutting it completely when it is fully charged. Without this facility you must keep checking the charger and turn it off when you start to hear fizzing or bubbling, which means it is fully charged and the electrolyte is starting to break down.

CHARGING SAFELY

Modern cars have so many electronic systems that the battery must be disconnected from the car before charging or the possible power surge may fry something expensive. It is safest to remove the battery from the car completely (see the previous section).

Charging should always be carried out in a well-ventilated place, away from possible sparks or naked flames because hydrogen is given off during charging. Connect the charger to the battery before plugging it in and make sure you connect the correct wires to the right terminals (red for positive or +, and black for negative or –).

It can take more than 24 hours to fully charge a totally flat battery but you may get enough power to start the car after a few hours. Unplug the charger from the mains before disconnecting it from the battery to reduce the risk of sparks. Disconnect one terminal at a time or you may short circuit yourself.

Do not try to jump-start with a battery charger because it is not designed for that sort of load. For jump-starting from another car, see Chapter 10.

10 THINGS TO REMEMBER

1 *Mishandling batteries can cause serious injury.*

2 *Try not to overload the battery when starting the car.*

3 *Do not leave unnecessary electrical items on when the engine is at idle or off.*

4 *If you have starting problems, check the battery.*

5 *Replace damaged batteries immediately.*

6 *Replace tired batteries as soon as you can and certainly before winter starts.*

7 *When removing or installing a battery in the car remember the earth lead is 'first out, last in'.*

8 *Dispose of batteries sensibly because they can cause injury and environmental damage.*

9 *Only recharge a battery with a charger intended for that type of battery.*

10 *Batteries give off hydrogen when being charged, which may explode if ignited.*

8

Cleaning

In this chapter you will learn:
- *why and how to keep your car clean*
- *how to tackle problem grime*
- *when you need professional help.*

It is not vanity to clean your car because it is a big investment and cleaning protects that investment. If you look after it, especially the interior, it will be worth more when you change it and you will not have to get it professionally valeted to get the best price for it.

It is easier to spot problems with paint or bodywork on a clean car because dirt hides small blemishes until they become big enough to show through it. In the winter, caked on grime contains road salt and holds moisture, acting as a rust-inducing poultice.

In addition, it is far more pleasant for you and, especially, your passengers to sit in a clean, fresh smelling car rather than a rubbish tip smelling of dogs and cigarettes (or worse).

Equipment

Avoid using mechanical car washes because their rotary brushes eventually dull the paintwork with millions of tiny scratches. However, you should still take care when hand cleaning it for the same reason – grit trapped in a sponge or cloth can do a lot of damage before you notice it. It is also sensible to keep car wash cloths, sponges and brushes separate from household cleaning items so they don't get used to wash a gritty floor or soaked in harsh household cleaners.

ESSENTIAL TOOLS

▶ *a 15-litre (three gallon) bucket*
▶ *bodywork brush*
▶ *bug sponge*
▶ *chamois leather*
▶ *two polishing cloths*
▶ *kitchen towel*
▶ *sponge and cloth for glass cleaner*
▶ *dry paintbrush*
▶ *vacuum cleaner*

USEFUL TOOLS

▶ *alloy wheel brush*
▶ *hose with trigger nozzle*
▶ *powerwasher (especially in rural areas)*

Save water

A hose is not a car cleaning essential and can waste a lot of water. If you have to use one, perhaps because the car is muddy, either get a nozzle that shuts off the water or turn the tap off when you are not using it.

HAND CARE

If you have sensitive skin, use rubber gloves as you will be handling products with all kinds of chemicals in them and do not know what nasties you are washing off the car. In winter, rubber gloves also make washing the car more comfortable.

CLEANING POWER

If you live in the country a powerwasher may be a car cleaning essential because in wet weather, especially at times when a lot of farm machinery is moving around, a rural car gets mud caked under wheel arches and a thin layer of it across the lower bodywork.

A powerwasher is likely to be more effective than a hose and so use less water getting this off, especially from underneath. If you try and wash mud off the bodywork with a bucket and sponge you merely spread it about and scratch the paint.

However, take care because even the domestic washers run at 1,500 psi, which is powerful enough to force water past seals. Wear safety glasses when using one because the dirt-laden water can ricochet at you with force.

Insight

One of the most useful car cleaning tools I've bought was a hook-shaped spray nozzle pipe for the powerwasher. This allows you to powerwash under the car and up inside wheel arches and prevented a repeat of a problem we had with a hatchback on which the handbrake cable ran along a channel in the centre of the floor. Unknown to me, mud built up in this channel, which caused no difficulties when it was wet. But when it froze, it stopped the brake fully releasing, though the brake handle moved normally. As a result I drove some distance wondering why the car felt sluggish and when I stopped to investigate, the overheated handbrake seized on. Dirt is not just an aesthetic problem.

SPONGE VS BRUSH

Most people use a cloth or sponge to wash the car but a purpose-made car washing brush with soft bristles is better because it does not trap grit so easily and is better at cleaning grilles and grooves. You can also get long-handled ones if you are short or your car is tall. If your car has intricate alloy wheels you may also need a small brush for spokes: several firms make wheel-cleaning brushes.

Buy a bug sponge from a car accessory shop. This is a sponge with a gently abrasive surface (don't use a washing up sponge) for getting squashed insects off glass and bodywork. When washing a car you should only have to use it on the most stubborn, baked-on bugs. You can also get wipes, like baby wet wipes, formulated to remove bugs and tar.

SHAMMY

A good chamois (pronounced 'sham-wah') leather, often called a shammy, makes drying the car off much easier. If you leave pools of water on the car it is likely to dry patchy as impurities in the water are left behind when it evaporates.

Modern shammy leather is nothing to do with the chamois animal but is made from sheep or calf skin from animals killed for meat. However, some synthetic shammies are as good as real leathers and last longer because they are not organic. Leather ones should only be rinsed in clean water, never soap or detergent, or they deteriorate.

POLISHING OFF

The best thing for applying wax or polish is stockinet, also known as mutton cloth because it was used to wrap sides of meat. You can buy this in big rolls in good car accessory shops and cut it to length. When you cut a piece, give it a good shake before getting in the car with it because it drops tiny bits of cut thread which are difficult to get out of carpets.

INTERIORS

For cleaning the interior, you need a vacuum cleaner with a thin nozzle plus a clean, dry 25 mm to 50 mm paintbrush for getting into nooks and crannies.

Cleaning products

There is a massive market in car cleaning preparations. It is often a false economy to buy cheap products because you need to use more of them and they can make the job harder. For example, cheap car shampoo often leaves a waxy bloom on the paint which must be polished off.

ESSENTIAL PRODUCTS

- *car shampoo*
- *car wax*
- *cleaner for plastic exterior trim*
- *glass cleaner*
- *interior shampoo*

USEFUL PRODUCTS

- *alloy wheel cleaner*
- *paint restorer*
- *engine degreaser (for older cars)*

WASHING

Car shampoo is worth buying because it is formulated for cars so is good at cleaning off road grime and shouldn't harm the paint or bodywork. Washing up liquid, in contrast, is usually bulked out with salt which encourages corrosion and can even get into the paint, showing as white rings after raindrops have dried on it. Some shampoos also have wax in them to top up the effects of hand waxing, where strong detergents may strip wax off the paint.

MAKING A SHINE

There is a difference between car wax and car polish. Strictly speaking, car wax merely puts a protective film over the paint, giving it a shine. Traditionally, polish is slightly abrasive and is intended to bring back the shine on tired paintwork, though now some manufacturers use 'polish' to describe what are really waxes. So read the bottle to see what you are getting.

Paint renovators (the best known is T-Cut) are gently abrasive, more so than polishes, and intended to take off a thin layer to remove tiny scratches. They should only be used occasionally to hide scratches or bring the shine back to very dull paint, for example on a car that has been through too many car washes or where the paint surface has oxidized.

Several firms now make nano-technology paint treatments. You usually use these after cleaning and polishing the car and they are claimed to fill the microscopic irregularities in the paint making the surface too smooth for dirt to stick. They make the paint feel smoother and seem to work – things that normally stick, like bird droppings, are washed off by rain.

BLACK STUFF

Many cars have black or grey plastic trim which is often textured. There are many products for cleaning this with, the best known being Back-to-Black and Armourall. These have a dual role in that they lift out dirt, or the white marks left by polish, from the textured surfaces and put a protective layer over the plastic to make it harder for new dirt to stick. But never use them on rubber floor mats or pedal rubbers because it makes them slippery.

CLEARLY BETTER

A good car glass cleaner is a wise buy because it cleans glass, inside and out, without leaving deposits that might stop wipers clearing the glass. Glass cleaning is covered in Chapter 5.

INTERIORS

Car interior cleaners that work with as little water as possible are useful to keep for coping with emergencies, like food getting ground into seats. The best ones use chemicals called surface reactants (**surfactants**), which get under the dirt and unstick it from the surface. One of the easiest to use is Autoglym's Interior Shampoo which can be used on carpets, fabrics and plastics and will even lift chocolate crumbs out of seat fabrics. However, with any interior cleaner, follow the instructions carefully and test it on a hidden area of fabric or carpet first.

Exterior cleaning

Top tip

While you wash the car look out for damage and tar spots that may need treating later.

WASHING

1 *Start by wetting the car down. You can use a hose for this but, if the car has no caked-on dirt, a watering can does it with less water. This is to soften deposits and remove loose, gritty particles. If you use a hose or powerwasher you start from the bottom up so you begin with the dirtiest areas and don't splatter mud on the cleaner bits. To powerwash mud out of wheel arches or from under the car, it is easier to use a hooked nozzle attachment. Take care to wash dislodged mud out of the backs of the wheels or it can unbalance them.*

2 *Only use the amount of shampoo the manufacturer recommends. If you use too much you may overdose it with the wax additive in the shampoo, which smears the paint and is hard to rinse off.*

3 *Wash from the top down, starting with the roof, then bonnet, front, sides and, finally the back and the wheels because they get the most grimy. If the sides are very dirty low down, clean all the upper parts of the car first, then do the lower parts after you've done the back. Change the water if it gets too mucky.*

4 *Don't forget to wash inside the door shuts, taking care not to wet the seats. Washing something you can't usually see may sound fussy, but this is the part of the car most likely to touch your clothes. In addition, dirt trapped here stays damp, increasing the risk of corrosion.*

5 *Rinse the car off with a hose, watering can or powerwasher.*

6 *Now shammy it, from the top down, using a bucket of clean water to rinse the leather frequently. Use the shammy to soak up any water trapped in joints or use a vacuum cleaner on blow to blast water out of these places.*

Try to use biodegradable cleaning products and, even then, do not wash the car where the run-off will go directly into waterways. Detergents are harmful to almost all aquatic life, which is why it is illegal to wash a car in a waterway in most countries.

WAXING

A car should only need waxing every six months – if water sprayed on the clean paint beads up, it doesn't need waxing.

The car must be dry or the wax/polish will smear and be difficult to remove, so if you are cleaning the inside, do that while you wait for the exterior to dry.

Work from the top down and put the polish on the cloth, not the car, for even coverage. It is best to do a panel at a time: if it is quick-drying you can usually start buffing it off one end soon after finishing applying it at the other. If not, apply it to, say, the roof and bonnet, then buff the roof. If you do a panel at a time you also won't be caught with a car covered in polish if it rains.

GLASS

If you use a car glass cleaner, do the windows now and don't forget the wiper blades. These cleaners remove any wax left by the shampoo and stop the wipers smearing. Sunroofs printed with a black perforated pattern should only be cleaned with water or a clear glass cleaner because the chalky ones won't come off the black.

Insight

Be careful to shake polishing cloths so dust from them does not blow into the car. There is nothing more annoying when you have spent time cleaning a car to find the interior spotted with powdery flecks of dry car wax or glass cleaner.

Saving work

Keep polish and chalky glass cleaner off black or grey plastic trim and window rubbers because it leaves white marks.

Clean these with products made for them and, if you use a spray product, squirt it onto a cloth for small bits of trim. On windy days do that for big bits, too, or the spray gets all over your nicely polished paint.

Exterior problems

TAR

Tar deposits on paintwork are unsightly, get onto clothes and
may even damage the paint. If you are washing the car, some
car waxes and polishes will lift tar, so try yours on a small area.
If it won't you can get cleaners and wipes to remove it, though
ordinary white spirit is as effective. If you have to use this, wash
the area and wax it afterwards. Most waxes make it harder for
tar to stick.

BIOLOGICAL WASTE

Bird mess is best cleaned off as soon as you can because it can
affect the paint. If it does eat into the paint, a paint renovator
might make minor damage harder to see, but if it is bad you'll
have to get professional help. Seagull mess can be particularly
damaging if left.

Manure can be a problem in rural areas. It is best if it is hosed
off as soon as possible because some of it sticks badly if allowed
to dry. If it has dried on, give it a soaking, preferably with car
shampoo in the water, and leave it to soften, then use a soft brush
and water, or a powerwasher, to remove it.

CHIPS AND SCRATCHES

Scratches and chips are only worth touching in if they are large.
Small scratches can be made less visible with a paint renovator.
Most modern paint systems have chip-resistant undercoats so
minor damage only needs to be touched in if bare metal is showing.
If you really can't live with chips, buy a touch-in kit and follow
the instructions. If you get a lot of stone chips you should question
whether you get too close to cars in front because something has to
be thrown at your car.

Interior cleaning

Keeping the interior clean and undamaged is important because when you sell the car, dealers are far less tolerant of expensive and difficult repairs to interior trim than they are to cosmetic damage outside.

METHOD

1 *Start by removing all your junk from the boot, floor and cubbies so you don't have to move it as you clean. This also gives you the chance to throw away the real rubbish.*

2 *If you are cleaning the windows with a chalky cleaner, do that first, so you can vacuum up the fallout. Try not to get the cleaner on the trim because it makes more work.*

3 *Go over large areas of plastic with the vacuum's duster brush. You are unlikely to be able to get this into smaller places so swap to the thin nozzle designed for getting between cushions. No matter how powerful your cleaner, this won't suck up dust held in place by static, so use a dry paintbrush to sweep dust out of crannies into the nozzle. Again, work from the top down.*

4 *Use the vacuum's upholstery attachment to do the seats, reverting to the thin nozzle to get between the cushions and into the recesses in the cushions. The thin nozzle also concentrates the suction to get hairs out of fabrics.*

5 *Do the boot and floor carpets last. Use the upholstery attachment first then use the thin nozzle for concentrated suction on stubborn areas.*

Top tip
Though sandy deposits in the carpet may not look too bad, they abrade the fibres so it is worth the effort to remove them.

6 *A good interior cleaner is worth using because it lifts dirt off the plastics and out of the fabrics and carpets, while most also deodorize. Test it on hidden areas first, use it according to the instructions and always clean a whole seat or carpet otherwise you'll get patches.*

INTERIOR TIPS

▶ *Never over-wet car seats or carpets, partly because they take a long time to dry out but also because they may shrink and the water might get into the electrics (many cars' engine management computers are under the front seats).*

▶ *Let carpets dry before you put mats back on them.*

▶ *Do not use interior cleaners on leather because they may dry it out. Use plain water, something formulated for leather or a cleaner recommended by the car manufacturer.*

▶ *Seatbelts should also only be cleaned with water because of the risk of chemicals weakening the fabric.*

▶ *The best thing to clean the instrument 'glass' and metallic interior trim with is a household multi-surface spray cleaner like Mr Sheen, but spray it onto a cloth so it won't go where it's not wanted.*

Interior problems

HAIR OF THE DOG

Pet hair can be very difficult to get out of carpets and fabric seats. The best thing to get them out with is a horse-grooming item called a rubber curry comb (see Plate 11), actually a disc of rubber serrations used for cleaning grooming brushes. You get them in saddlers' shops (try online if you don't live near one) but only get a rubber one because a metal or plastic one won't do the job. You sweep this across the fabric and it pulls the hairs out, either trapping them on the comb or leaving them to be vacuumed up. A window squeegee will also do this, but not as well.

Really stubborn hairs may let go if lightly sprayed with a surfactant interior cleaner. But if all else fails, repeatedly dabbing with a rolled up piece of sticky tape (sticky side out) may do it.

CHOCOLATE

Chocoholics never notice how much they drop until it is ingrained in the seat fabric. Use a blunt edge, like an ice-lolly stick or plastic spoon, to scrape off as much as possible, then use a surfactant cleaner to remove the rest. Better still, ban chocolate from the car.

> **Insight**
>
> Do not ignore chocolate that looks as if it has sunk too deep into the fabric to do any harm. When it gets hot it can mark light-coloured clothes.

MOULD

It is pointless treating mould until you have established the cause. If it is obviously from forgotten food, you have only yourself to blame, but if carpets are damp, the source of the dampness must be traced. Check it is not something daft, like leaving wet umbrellas in the car.

Unfortunately, tracing leaks in cars is difficult because the water may come in far from where it gathers. If you can't find anything, get a garage to check because they often know where particular cars leak.

Once the leak is eliminated, give the area a good clean with interior cleaner. If you can leave the car with the windows open, especially on a hot day, it speeds up drying. If the mould persists, you may have to use a mould killer, but try it on a hidden area first.

Unfortunately, if damp and mould have been left too long the carpets and underlay may have rotted and the only answer is to replace them.

> **Insight**
>
> Those of us with dogs and horses soon learn the value of some form of boot protection. If you need to put anything wet or dirty into the car, including sports gear and wellies, invest in a rubber boot mat. Many car manufacturers' accessory ranges include boot liners or tray mats, with upturned edges, that keep mud and water contained. Bootliners can seem expensive but they are a lot cheaper than replacing a rotted carpet. Avoid throwing wet coats onto the back seat. If you have nowhere else to put them, fold them so the coat's dry interior is against the seat.

If you have to remove tough stains like ink, tar, fat, grease or paint from the interior, do not use solvents or strong household cleaners. Almost all the materials in a car are synthetic or have synthetics beneath them, which may be seriously affected by solvents. Even a natural fibre seat fabric has plastic foam underneath and may have synthetic stitching, so you might get the paint out of the cloth but find the foam or stitching melts.

Some inks, most fats and some greases will come out with a surfactant cleaner, but if those fail, seek professional help.

The professionals

There are times when expertise and products only available to the trade are needed to save or restore a car's appearance. That is when you need the services of a professional car valeter or a **Smart repairer** (see below) – some businesses combine them both.

LIKE NEW

A proper car valet goes way beyond a simple car clean. A good valet service leaves the interior looking and smelling like new through the use of specialist knowledge, the right cleaning products and attention to detail.

They are certainly the people to call if ordinary interior cleaners won't remove stains and for emergencies like spilt paint, vomit or milk-soaked seats. Indeed, with such emergencies it is sensible to call them to ask what you should do until you can get the car to them. Once they have cleaned it they can deodorize the car by using a device called a fogger which fills the car with a mist that neutralizes smells.

Buying and selling

It is worth considering a professional valet when you buy or sell a used car. When you buy a used car and want to get rid of the previous owner's dirt and smells, a professional valet can give you the 'new car' sensation. When you sell the car, especially if you haven't been fastidious about inner cleanliness, a valet creates a good impression and may get back more than it cost. Even if you trade it in to a dealer, it means they can give you the best deal because they don't need to get it cleaned.

SMART STUFF

Smart repairs are where a small repair is made to just the area damaged. So, instead of replacing the entire centre console they invisibly repair just the mobile phone bracket holes or they fill and paint stone chips instead of respraying the whole bonnet. They are almost always cost effective, and in the case of accident damage may be cheaper than your **insurance excess** or losing a no claims bonus.

Externally, Smart repairs are ideal for stone chips, scratches and other minor paint damage, small dents, damage to plastic trim and some plastic bumper repairs (they can weld some plastics but not all).

Internal repairs are often ingenious. Holes in plastics are filled with a colour-matched filler then a tool is used to give the surface a texture to match its surroundings. Cigarette burns in fabrics are filled by gluing in what looks like tumble dryer fluff to make a repair that is difficult to see even if you know where it is. They can also restore the colour and feel of leather and carpets and can sometimes weld cracked plastic components.

There are also companies that specialize in restoring damaged or corroded alloy wheels, which is much cheaper than replacing them.

10 THINGS TO REMEMBER

1 Cleaning protects the value of your investment in the car.

2 Consider the environment by using the minimum water and choosing biodegradable products.

3 Buy a powerwasher if your car gets caked on dirt.

4 Cheap cleaning products are usually false economy. Use all cleaning products according to instructions and test interior cleaners on fabrics before use.

5 Keep all cleaning cloths free of grit.

6 When hosing or powerwashing a dirty car work from the bottom up.

7 When washing and polishing, work from the top down.

8 Rinse as you go along in warm weather.

9 Use the vacuum cleaner's crevice tool for extra suction on carpets.

10 Never get seats and carpets too wet.

9

Servicing

In this chapter you will learn:
- *why and when cars need servicing*
- *how to choose a garage*
- *how to complain*
- *how to get an MOT.*

Cars are complex machines and though a lot has been done to reduce the servicing they need, they still need it in order to work efficiently and remain safe. It used to be common for cars to need servicing every 5,000 or 6,000 miles, though usually this was an oil change at, say, 6,000 and a full service at 12,000. But oils and oil filters have been improved to remove the need for an intermediate change so now a 12,000 mile service interval is normally a minimum. For many cars the service interval is even longer because many things that used to need adjustment have either been made self-adjusting or harder wearing.

But even with all this technology, various fluids need replacing because they can no longer do their job. Engine oil absorbs a lot of impurities from the combustion process, all lubricants get 'tired' from the constant thrashing around and brake fluid absorbs moisture from the air, increasing the risk of brake fade. Mechanical parts also wear, with brake shoes getting worn down, drive belts getting stretched and worn, nuts and bolts working loose and things suffering physical damage as a result of driver error or road debris.

You could leave it until something goes wrong, but that something could be life threatening and if you replace, say, a camshaft drive belt before it breaks, it avoids the expensive engine repairs its failure would have caused. In addition, as things go out of adjustment the car runs less efficiently, so you increase day-to-day running costs with higher fuel consumption, increased tyre wear and the need to top up the oil. This also increases the car's impact on the environment.

It is easy to get upset about the cost of servicing because it is a big bill. But for most motorists it is a once a year event and though it might hurt the pocket at the time, it is nothing compared to the annual cost of fuel, taxation, depreciation and, for some drivers, insurance. In addition, unlike those things, it keeps you safe. Many people complain about the labour costs of car servicing, but forget this reflects the training technicians have to go through along with the considerable cost of equipment. In many places the hourly rate for even a prestige marque dealership compares favourably with getting a washing machine serviced in spite of the far greater complexity and responsibility of the work.

When you are checking prices for servicing and repair, remember the difference between an estimate and a quote. An estimate is what the garage thinks it is likely to cost and it is best to set a maximum above which they can't go without consulting you. A quote, which should be written, explains what work will be done and parts required and gives a price for the work.

How often?

Your car's handbook, or a service book enclosed with it, explains service intervals. This can be difficult to understand because some manufacturers include variables for extreme use, like the need for more frequent services if you use the car for towing, in extreme temperatures or in dusty conditions. However, by that they may mean towing several times a week or driving your off-roader through the dust-laden heat of the Mojave Desert. If you are in doubt, ask a franchised dealer or the car manufacturer's customer service department.

LEEWAY

New and used car warranties always demand that the car is serviced to the manufacturer's requirements. The warranty conditions usually state how much leeway you are allowed, which in most cases is 1,000 miles or a month, but check because they vary. If you fail to comply with this they can refuse to pay for repairs, especially if it can be shown that a lack of maintenance could have contributed to a failure.

One thing it is important to check is whether a time interval is also laid down. Many manufacturers say the car must be serviced, say, at 20,000 miles or annually. This means if you do 40,000 miles a year you need to get it serviced twice a year at 20,000, but if you only do 10,000 miles a year you need to get it serviced annually even though it hasn't done the mileage. This is because things still deteriorate over time even if the car is parked. Indeed, some things may even deteriorate more quickly, like an exhaust that never gets hot enough to prevent chemical-laden moisture condensing inside.

SERVICE INDICATORS

A few cars, like those made by the Volkswagen Group and BMW, have sophisticated service interval indicators. These take data on how the car is used and adjust the service interval accordingly, telling you when one is required. So, a car used for a lot of short journeys, rarely reaching the engine's full working temperature, may need servicing more often than one used for regular long trips.

However, some so-called service indicators are little more than an odometer that lets you know when the set mileage is up, so, unlike the VW and BMW ones, it won't tell you an annual service is due if you haven't done the mileage.

Services vary

All car manufacturers publish full service schedules for their cars
of what needs doing when. Some include these in their handbooks.
This recognizes the fact that not everything needs doing at every
service and is also why some services cost more than others.

A typical schedule for a petrol-engined car with a 12,000 mile
service interval says the oil is changed at every service but the air
conditioning air filter is changed every 24,000 miles and the brake
linings inspected every 36,000. Then at 48,000 you can expect a big
bill because they also change the engine air filter, inspect steering
joint seals, adjust the drive belts and replace the **sparkplugs**. This
carries on through the car's life with the manufacturer laying down
times or mileages for the replacement of drive belts, the draining
and replacement of coolant and brake fluid, and so on.

Intervals

Services are carried out, say, 12,000 miles after the previous
service, so a car may have its 48,000 mile service when the
odometer is showing other mileage. Let's say you bought this
12,000 mile service interval car as a used car with 9,500 miles on

the clock and the dealer carried out a service then. Its next service is now due at 21,500 miles, not 24,000. If you want to make it easier to remember when services are due, you can bring it back into line by having the next few services a little later, so if the manufacturer says you have 1,000 miles leeway on servicing you could get the next done at just under 22,500.

On the record

We have seen that warranties depend on regular servicing and that what needs to be done to the car changes with its age, so these are two good reasons for keeping a service record. If you get the garage to stamp a service book showing it has been serviced regularly, you shouldn't have any trouble when making warranty claims. It also helps to make a note on the page when something important is changed, like the camshaft drive belt, not least so you don't get it changed unnecessarily because you can't remember if it was done.

Better still, keep all the receipts so you have a record of exactly what has been done. This also means if a replacement part fails early, you can go back to the garage and show them when it was fitted. Most franchised dealers warranty replacement parts for a year and reputable independents would cover them for several months at least.

Finally, a service record makes the car easier to sell and helps it retain its value. The new owner can see, especially if you retain receipts, that you have cared for it and it gives them a record of when jobs were last done.

Insight

It is easier to keep track of things if you split your 'car file' into sections. At least have one section for bills and one for legally required documents, like the registration document and insurance paperwork.

Doing it yourself

If you know about cars there is no reason why you shouldn't do all the servicing yourself. But you will almost certainly have problems with warranty claims and you must be sure you are doing the work to the manufacturer's full schedule. It is wise to buy either a manufacturer's workshop manual or an independently produced one, like the well-known Haynes series.

Some people who own an older car that needs an intermediate oil change service, do the oil and filter change themselves but use a garage for the major service to ensure everything that should be checked is seen by an expert. How you do an oil change is outside the scope of this book. If you are going to do this you must have a safe area to do it in, the correct tools and the facilities to safely dispose of the oil.

If you do service work yourself it is essential you keep bills to prove you have done it and make a record of when work was done. If you don't you won't know when the next service is due.

However, there are little things you can do yourself. Filling the washer bottle before it goes for service or rotating the wheels are easy enough jobs, but remember to tell the garage so they don't repeat the work and charge you for it.

Choosing a garage

Many people still believe that if they own a new car they must get it serviced at a franchised dealer to retain the warranty, but under EU law manufacturers can only require that the car must be serviced according to the manufacturer's schedule.

EASIER WARRANTY CLAIMS

Of course, if you have a warranty claim you may have to prove the correct servicing has been done, where a franchised dealer would have a record of it. Indeed, dealers in a franchised network often have computer access to records of work done at other dealerships, so you shouldn't have problems getting warranty work done if a fault develops away from home. In addition, many manufacturers give you more leeway on warranty claims if you have had the car serviced by their network, so they might forgive the odd late service or pay for a repair when the car is just outside the warranty period.

FRANCHISED DEALERS

The other benefits of using franchised dealers are:

▶ *You know they use original equipment parts, which are usually warranted for a year.*
▶ *Their technicians are factory trained.*
▶ *They have the latest diagnostic technology.*
▶ *They are regularly updated on potential trouble in the cars.*
▶ *They have instant access to a wealth of knowledge about the marque.*
▶ *If anything goes wrong you can go to the manufacturer if you don't get satisfaction locally.*
▶ *They usually offer collection and delivery, a lift to or from the garage or a courtesy car.*
▶ *All accept credit cards where some small garages want cash.*

The drawbacks to franchised garages are:

▶ *They are sometimes more expensive because they have to maintain a large showroom.*
▶ *Some appear to have little time for owners of older cars.*
▶ *Most routinely use the high specification oils required for current models on older cars that do not need them.*
▶ *They can get very busy at peak times of year, like the plate change periods when the majority of new cars are sold and then need servicing a year later.*
▶ *The dealer serving your area may be a long way from your home or work.*

INDEPENDENT GARAGES

The benefits of independent garages are:

▶ *They are often cheaper because they have lower overheads.*
▶ *They depend on a good reputation locally to get work.*
▶ *They may be closer to your home or work.*
▶ *They usually have more experience of working on older cars.*
▶ *They will use cheaper oils and non-original parts on older cars if you want them to.*

The drawbacks of independents are:

▶ *Warranty claims on new cars may not be so easy.*
▶ *They may not be able to offer franchised dealer levels of service, like courtesy cars.*
▶ *They may not have the latest equipment.*
▶ *Few use menu pricing (see below).*
▶ *They do not have the manufacturer backup on technical information and notification of potential problems.*
▶ *You do not have recourse to the manufacturer if their service is poor.*

COMPARING PRICES

The general view is that franchises charge more than independents, but this isn't always so. If you compare prices make sure you compare like with like. As we've seen, each service involves different amounts of work, so comparing service bills isn't always fair.

If you ask for labour charges, the independent will almost always be cheaper but many franchised dealers (and some independents) now work on what the trade calls 'menu pricing'. This means for certain jobs they have a set price, like a dish on a restaurant's menu, so those jobs cost you the same whether it goes without a hitch or takes them 30 minutes to free a stuck nut. If you pay by the hour, the stuck nut increases costs. However, the menu charge is usually labour only and there are parts on top.

The best advice when seeking prices is to ask how much a 20,000 mile service on your car would cost and check what that includes. Ask the independent whether they use original equipment parts, what warranty they give and whether they have the diagnostic equipment necessary. A franchised dealer automatically plugs your car into electronic diagnostic equipment to ensure everything is running correctly but a poor backstreet garage might only do it if they have trouble tracing a fault and then send it to a bigger firm and charge you a mark-up on what they paid.

TRADE BODIES

If you decide to go to an independent, see what trade bodies they belong to. The Retail Motor Industry Federation (RMIF) ensures minimum standards and offers arbitration if anything goes wrong. Its website, at www.rmif.co.uk, also has a search facility for member garages in your area. The Scottish Motor Trade Association (SMTA) does a similar job in Scotland, and also has a garage search facility on its website at www.smta.co.uk.

Some Trading Standards departments run 'Good Garage' schemes so it may be worth contacting your local one or looking on its website. If Trading Standards isn't listed in your phone book it may be under the county council or equivalent. You can also do a postcode search to find your local Trading Standards at www.tradingstandards.gov.uk.

PHONE A FRIEND

There are good and bad garages among both franchises and independents, so ask around. You get some franchised dealers who treat customers and their cars badly, giving as little customer service as they can without losing the franchise, but there are others who go beyond what manufacturers demand. There are some very good independents, especially the classic family-owned village garages who rely on a good reputation locally and provide many of the extras dealers do, like courtesy cars, but there are also some serious crooks and you only find out by trial and error.

A point of courtesy

If you accept a courtesy car, check the insurance. Garages sometimes expect you to get it covered under your own car insurance, so see what cover you have on your policy. Most fully comprehensive insurance only gives you third party cover when driving other people's cars, so you pay for damage to or replacement of the car you are driving. A few make exceptions for courtesy cars but most require you to notify them of its details, which you need in advance from the garage.

Some insurers used to cover courtesy cars for free a few times a year as long as the car was not greatly more powerful or valuable than your own, but fewer now do that. If you have to pay, check to see whether your insurer or the garage are cheaper.

If you insure the courtesy car, make sure it is the one the garage gave you details of when you collect it and if it isn't insist they cover it on their own insurance and give you a note to that effect, or that they at least pay for your call to your insurer to change the details.

If you have a UK photo driving licence you must take both parts of the licence to the garage, not just the photocard, because the paper part records any driving offences. Garages and car hire companies have to insist on seeing the original paper part because it is required by their insurers and protects them if it turns out you could not legally drive the car.

COURTESY PAYS

Be courteous to the garage, too. The earlier you get the car in, the sooner they can get to work on it. Tell them of any special needs and try not to deliver it in a really disgusting state: nobody wants to work on a car you've just driven through a manure-covered farmyard. If you want the service book stamped, hand it to the service receptionist and if the car has locking wheel nuts for the alloy wheels, leave the key somewhere obvious in the car and tell the receptionist where it is. Also make sure it has a reasonable amount of fuel because they may need to run it for certain tests or to road test it.

Above all, if you can't get the car in for any reason, call them as soon as possible. That way they can make best use of their workshop time and may be able to help another motorist with a problem. They are more likely to fit you in at short notice in future if you have been reasonable to them. You are more likely to get good service from a garage if you build a good relationship with them.

Keeping costs down

There are little ways of keeping costs down without skimping on servicing.

KEEP CONTROL

Make it clear that if they find anything wrong you want to know about it before they do the work. That way you can discuss the work, agree prices and not be charged for things you can do yourself, like replacing a wiper blade. It also means you can spread the cost by getting essential work done today and waiting until next month's pay cheque to book it in for less important items.

LEAVE IT OUT

Check beforehand what you are paying for and if you think anything is unnecessary, ask them to leave it and reduce the bill. For example, many garages valet the car as part of a service, but if it is clean, ask them to leave it and knock a bit off the bill.

OIL FIELDS

If you have an ageing car it might not be worth using high tech synthetic oils, so ask them to use a cheaper mineral one. Some people buy a suitable oil from a service station or retailer and tell the garage to use that to ensure they are not overcharged. Some garages take liberties with oil pricing, for example, charging as if they buy it in litre cans from the local petrol station rather than in bulk at a discount.

WASHERS

Another common way to add a few pounds to the bill is to top up the washer bottle and charge for a full bottle of washer fluid. Sometimes this is because they are supplied with a kit of service items by the manufacturer which includes this. So, fill the bottle to the brim before the car goes in and query it if it is on the bill and the bottle of fluid isn't in the car.

CHECK THE BILL

Go through the bill before you pay, querying anything you don't understand. Be polite but firm and make it clear that it's not because you don't trust them (even if you don't) but because you want to understand what has been done to your car. If they gave you an estimate for the cost of the work and it is substantially over, demand an explanation and haggle.

CHECK THE CAR

When you collect the car, have a look over it to check it is in good order and has things like a new oil filter (it will be clean).

Repairs

The difference between servicing and repairs is that servicing is preventative while repairs are as a result of a problem.

Always think carefully before soldiering on with a minor fault. If it is a safety related item you must get it sorted out as soon as possible and some serious safety related things, like faulty brakes, mean it is not safe to drive at all so it must be transported to the garage.

If you are alerted to a fault by a warning light, check what action the handbook suggests. In general if it is a red light it is more serious than if it is an orange or yellow one. Ignoring such warnings can lead to serious damage. A coolant level light might mean nothing more than a top up but ignoring it could result in a wrecked engine because the system is empty as a result of a leak. If the car is under warranty, they may reject a claim where they can show you have ignored a warning light or left a minor fault until it has become more serious.

However, with something like a loose bit of trim or an electric mirror that needs a helping hand, you might be able to live with it until an imminent service comes round.

If it is under warranty, let the garage know when you book it in. It is easiest to get this sort of work done at a franchised dealer because their opinion that it is a warranty job is almost always accepted.

GET A QUOTE

For major repairs outside a warranty you might want to get quotes from more than one garage, but make sure you compare like with like. Ask:

► *Are they using original equipment parts?*
► *Does this quote include labour and VAT?*
► *Is it a set price or is it an estimate of the likely labour time?*

- *Is there a warranty on the repairs?*
- *Do they accept credit cards? (Important for big jobs.)*

Again, some garages do common repairs on a menu-pricing basis so can tell you the exact cost of, say, replacing a clutch, while others charge an hourly rate so it costs more if they have problems. Try to get a written quote. Trading Standards also suggests setting a maximum cost they should not go above without consulting you, which is sensible especially if the car is of low value where the repair might cost more than it is worth.

Top tip

Don't agree to leave the car so they can work on it when they can fit it in, but book it in to be done by a certain time so they can't keep you waiting.

Some firms also specialise in certain types of repairs, like electrical, power steering, gearboxes or air conditioning. Because they specialize they may be cheaper for those jobs than more general garages.

Recalls

Recalls are where the car manufacturer has found a design fault or a component fault that affects a model or range of cars. Manufacturers are legally bound to institute a full recall for faults where there is a risk of serious mechanical failure or safety problems. They then work with the DVLA to contact all registered owners of affected cars so you should receive a notice through the post telling you what the problem is and what to do.

Don't panic, unless the letter stresses there is immediate danger, because often these faults are found in only a limited number of cars or in certain extreme circumstances. But, equally, do not ignore these warnings because they wouldn't engage in such an expensive process if there were not just cause. These repairs are free even if the car is out of warranty.

There is a second level of 'recall', though this is officially a 'notification', where there is a potential problem that is relatively minor but still a quality issue. In these circumstances the manufacturer may let owners know to look out for the problem and take the car in if it occurs, but more often they alert dealers to remedy it when the car comes in for service.

Insight

Some manufacturers err a long way on the cautious side with safety related recalls while others take a limited view of what constitutes a safety issue. For example, Toyota once recalled a particular model worldwide for a fault that only occurred below −20°C. Yet one European manufacturer refused to yield to pressure that a bonnet catch that was prone to fail if not lubricated properly was a safety related issue, even though people had had bonnets block their view while driving.

Testing times

Almost every developed country has a road worthiness test but the age at which they start, frequency and issues covered varies considerably. Some motorists view testing as a costly nuisance but it has removed the most lethal cars from our roads and means that even if a car is serviced by the owner, it is regularly inspected by an expert.

The UK's **MOT** (Ministry of Transport) test is fairly typical and must be carried out annually on all cars over three years old. It is illegal to drive a car more than three years old without a valid MOT unless you are driving to a test centre or repair garage with an appointment. If you do that, make sure the garage has logged your appointment.

The test can be carried out up to a calendar month before it is due and the MOT computer dates it from the end of the old certificate or the car's third birthday. However, if the car fails its MOT, any previous certificate is no longer valid, even if it has a few weeks left to run, and as this information is now stored electronically, any policeman who stops you can check that.

You can either get the test done at a test centre independent of a garage or at a garage that also does servicing. Some people believe that a garage that knows it is doing the repairs is more likely to fail the car, but failure is failure and you're going to have to get the work done anyway. Also, garages can do a retest for free if they are doing the repairs and many do MOTs at a discounted rate if it is done with a service. If a car fails the test and you return it to the same test centre within the time stated on the failure certificate, the centre can check just that item and charge a reduced fee.

The MOT is the responsibility of the Vehicle Operator Services Agency and you can find out more about them and find local test centres on their website at www.vosa.gov.uk or www.direct.gov.uk. MOTs are registered on a central database so insurance companies, police and others can check the car has one. You can't tax a car without an MOT, and insurance may be invalid if you do not have one.

Top tip

Many garages that carry out an MOT remind you prior to its anniversary. I also note it on my computer and phone diaries because they automatically alert me to the approaching date.

Check the car over yourself before an MOT because it is pretty obvious it will fail if lights don't work or the tyres are illegal.

Complaints

Under the UK's Sale of Goods and Services Act (and common law in Scotland) a garage must work on your car with reasonable care and skill, finish the job in a reasonable time or the time agreed and do it at a reasonable price or the price agreed. They are also bound to take reasonable care of it, so if it is damaged in their possession they are liable for repairs. Trading law varies considerably from state to state, so check your rights locally.

HOW TO COMPLAIN

If you feel you have cause for complaint, the first step is to tell the garage. Nine times out of ten they will sort things out straight away, but if they do not, put your complaint in writing.

If a fault hasn't been fixed, take the car back to them as soon as possible. If you can't do that you must still let them know as soon as you can that the problem is still there. If they won't accept liability, put it in writing giving a date by which time you want it fixed. If it is serious or expensive you might want to get an independent report from a vehicle engineer or your motoring organization. If the garage refuses to take action you might have to get the fault repaired at another garage and claim the cost back through a trade association or court.

If repairs are not finished in a reasonable time or at the time agreed, talk to the garage and agree a finish date. If they procrastinate or fail to meet that date you might have to take the car away, but you have to pay for any work completed.

PAYING UNDER PROTEST

One difficulty with complaining about work on a car is that the garage has a legal right to retain it until disputed work has been paid for, for example, if work was done without your authorization or is more expensive than you were led to expect. In these circumstances all you can do is pay and make it clear by writing on your copy of the bill, and theirs, that it is 'paid under protest'. You must also put your complaint in writing to the garage and will then have to get your money back through a trade association or the courts.

GETTING HELP

Local Citizens' Advice Bureaux and Trading Standards departments can help (see 'Choosing a garage' earlier in the chapter). Small claims are pursued through the Sheriff Court in Scotland and County Courts in the rest of the UK and the Trading Standards website has information and forms for that.

If your complaint is with a franchised dealer, contact the car manufacturer's customer service department or the Society of Motor Manufacturers and Traders on 020 7235 7000 or at www.smmt.co.uk/consumeradvice. If a garage is a member of the Retail Motor Industry Federation, they offer an arbitration arrangement through the National Conciliation and Arbitration Service. Contact the RMIF on 020 7580 9122 or at www.rmif.co.uk. The Scottish Motor Trade Association also has a conciliation service and can be contacted on 0131 331 5510 or via www.smta.co.uk.

Warranty work

If you have a dispute over warranty work, especially whether something should have been covered, read the warranty document thoroughly. This should lay down what is covered and what to do in the event of a dispute. Most warranties have some sort of arbitration set-up but remember that a warranty is in addition to your legal rights, not in place of them, so talk to Trading Standards if you think someone is using a warranty to avoid giving you what you are entitled to under law.

10 THINGS TO REMEMBER

1   *Servicing keeps your car safe and efficient and is a warranty requirement.*

2   *To keep the warranty valid you must have the car serviced to the manufacturer's schedule but do not have to have it done at a franchised dealer.*

3   *Check your handbook or service schedule to see how often it must be done.*

4   *Keep a service record, preferably with the bills.*

5   *Using a franchised dealer makes warranty claims easier and ensures original parts are used.*

6   *An independent garage may be cheaper.*

7   *Make sure when comparing prices that you compare like with like, for example, that prices quoted include VAT.*

8   *Get quotes for repairs, not estimates.*

9   *Set a maximum cost for work above which they must contact you before starting.*

10 *Make a note of when your car needs its MOT.*

10

Breakdowns

In this chapter you will learn:
- *what to keep in the car*
- *about breakdown safety*
- *about wheel changing*
- *how to push and jump-start*.

Breakdowns are at best inconvenient and at worst life threatening and they almost always happen at the most inconvenient times in the worst places and nastiest weather.

You can minimize the risk of breakdown by making the regular checks described in Chapter 5 and making sure the car is properly serviced. Don't 'leave it until later' if you spot a potential fault or think something isn't quite right.

If your car isn't under warranty breakdown cover, join a breakdown organization, as explained in Chapter 1. Basic breakdown cover is cheap and even the most expensive and comprehensive packages are still cheaper than the police duty garage's fee for recovery from a UK motorway is likely to be. Breakdown cover is also not only cheaper than a garage call-out but you know who to call no matter what time of day or where you are.

Essential equipment

At least have:

- *high visibility vest**
- *torch*
- *jack and **wheel brace** (except on cars with no spare wheel)*
- *screwdriver.*

Preferably have:

- *small set of spanners*
- *pliers*
- *insulating tape and fuses*
- *warning triangle**
- *first aid kit and fire extinguisher**
- *spare bulbs**
- *waterp...*

*

Ma_____and that
you_____t do not
be te_____y on
cars_____of metal
that_____bumps
and t_____ssiles
smash_____ 12.)

If you_____the
car's br_____brace
with an_____g you can use as an
extensio_____ car's brace's handle.

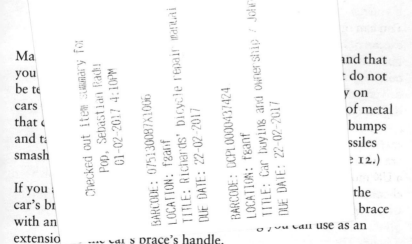

Checked out item summary for
Pop, Sebastian Radu
01-02-2017 4:10PM

BARCODE: 0751300B7X1006
LOCATION: fganf
TITLE: Richards' bicycle repair manual /
DUE DATE: 22-02-2017

BARCODE: DCP10000437424
LOCATION: fganf
TITLE: Car buying and ownership / John H
DUE DATE: 22-02-2017

TOOLS

It's also wise to add a few other tools to the basics supplied with the car because it is daft to be stuck for the sake of a loose screw. You only need a basic kit small enough to be kept in a large pencil case. Buy either a double-ended screwdriver, which has a single blade that has a flat head at one end and crosshead at the other, or a multi-bladed set. Add a small set of spanners and an adjustable one that can tackle nut sizes not catered for in the set or be used when you need to hold a bolt steady while doing up the nut. A pair of pliers, insulating tape and a small knife are also useful. Another solution is a multi-tool device that has many of these tools folding into a single handle.

Most cars have provision in the fusebox to keep one of each type of fuse used, but if yours hasn't, keep some spares in a small plastic box (a 35 mm film canister is ideal).

PERSONAL SAFETY

A few cars now come with high visibility reflective vests in their toolkits because in many countries these are a legal requirement if you get out of a car at the scene of an accident. They are also a very sensible thing to carry for emergency situations and are very cheap life savers if you buy them from places like builders' merchants. Posh cars also often include a pair of heavy cotton gloves in the toolkit, which fastidious or sensitive-skinned drivers might want to copy. Alternatively, keep moist wipes in the car.

TRIANGLES

Some, mostly German, cars come with a warning triangle, which is compulsory in some countries to warn other drivers of an obstruction. They are a wise thing to carry and should be set up about 50 metres behind the car and further back if you are round a bend. The trouble with triangles is that you can always hold it in front of you as you walk away from the car, drawing drivers' attention to the fact you are there, but you have to walk back hoping they take notice of the triangle by the road. That is one reason why the Highway Code no longer recommends their use on motorways, though anything placed even close behind your car to draw attention to the fact it has stopped is a good idea.

LIGHT

All this is wasted if you can't see what you're doing in a dark country road, so keep a torch in the car but put it in the glovebox, or somewhere else in the cabin, so you can find it before getting out of the car to help you seek out tools. Use alkaline or lithium ion batteries because these don't run down when they're not used, unlike rechargeables.

COLD AND WET

If you don't want to carry a coat in the car, at least keep a compact emergency waterproof with the tools. Outdoor clothing shops stock basic waterproofs that fold up into a small pack. In cold weather take appropriate clothing even on short trips because a car quickly gets cold once the engine stops. If you are driving in extreme weather, or through a remote area, it is sensible to carry snacks because your body can't keep warm without fuel. If you regularly drive in remote, cold areas consider keeping at least one foil 'space blanket' in the car, which can be bought cheaply in outdoor pursuit shops. In hot weather, take a bottle of water. Women wearing shoes unsuitable for walking should keep a more sensible pair in the car in case they have to walk to get help: mobile phones don't work everywhere.

What to do

The most important thing when something goes wrong in a car is not to make the situation worse. You want to minimize damage to the car without increasing the risk to you, your passengers and other road users. That means not ignoring the early signs of something going wrong, like a warning light, odd noises or the car behaving strangely, but not panicking and over-reacting so you do something others don't expect. So don't suddenly swerve towards the side of the road or stop on a blind bend to change a wheel. Driving to a safe place might wreck the tyre, but getting hit by a truck does a lot more damage.

Insight

A Highways Agency Traffic Officer once told me he had recently come across someone trying to change a wheel in the outside lane of a busy motorway. Amazingly, he and his colleagues said that was not an unusual occurrence, but what made this case exceptional was that the man's children were playing around the car! While you want to minimize damage, safety must always be your priority. That driver endangered his family and everyone else using the motorway who would not have expected a stationary car and children to be there.

There is a temptation if something catastrophic happens, like the engine suddenly cutting out, to hit the hazard warning lights. Only do this if you are sure it will not confuse people and you do not need to indicate your intention to pull across the road. Even if the engine cuts out, you still have some forward momentum to carry you to reasonable safety, as long as you depress the clutch or slip an automatic into neutral. But you usually get enough warning of something going wrong to pull over.

Hard shoulders

Motorways and many dual carriageways have hard shoulders for emergency use. As soon as you stop on the hard shoulder, use your hazard warning lights and remember it is a dangerous place because of the risk of other drivers following you onto the shoulder, not realizing you have stopped. There are said to be more fatal accidents on the hard shoulder than on the live carriageways. If you can, get out of the car on the passenger side, away from the traffic.

Even if you know it is something you can deal with yourself, let the authorities know you are there. On motorways and some major A-roads there are marker posts which bear a number and a sign showing the direction to the nearest emergency phone (see Plate 13). Even if you have a mobile, it is better to use these free phones because they show the police or Highways Agency control room where you are. It is common for people to think they are on, say, the M1 when they are on the M6.

Before you go to the phone, check you have all the things you need.

▶ *Write down the number on the nearest marker post because that gives a unique location on the motorway.*
▶ *Find your breakdown organization membership number.*
▶ *Check you know your car make, model and registration number.*

Give the controller your details, the nature of the problem and say if you are a woman travelling alone or if you have special needs – like a disability, children or animals in the car. They will call your breakdown organization. Listen to any safety advice the controller gives and don't hang up until they tell you to in case they do not have all the necessary information.

SAFETY

If you must work on the traffic side of the car, think carefully about how close you will be to the moving traffic. Even a glancing blow from a car at motorway speeds could be fatal. If it looks unsafe, ask the motorway control for help or call your breakdown organization who have the advantage of a large truck with flashing lights or the option of towing you off the motorway.

··

Top tip

Because of the risk of drivers colliding with the car on the hard shoulder, it is best for everyone to get out and wait on the verge, well away from the road. If there is a barrier, get the other side of it. Never sit on a barrier with your legs on

(Contd)

the traffic side of it because if anything hits you, it crushes your legs against the barrier. If you are working on the car and have passengers, get them to watch the traffic while you work so they can raise the alarm if anything endangers you.

REJOINING THE ROAD

When rejoining the carriageway afterwards, match your speed to the traffic's by accelerating along the hard shoulder, with your right indicator on. Check your mirrors, not just looking at the inside lane but the next one over as well, in case anyone is moving over in spite of you indicating your intention to move out.

Ordinary roads

On ordinary roads, use your hazards and get off the road if you can but take care if you pull off the tarmac not to pull onto soft ground or into hidden obstacles or ditches, especially at night.

If you are in an unsafe place, like on a bend, think carefully about whether it is better to risk further damage by driving on to a safer location.

Top tip
It may be sensible to ask a passenger to go down the road and wave down anyone approaching the scene too fast, or at least to keep an eye on the traffic as you work on the car.

CALLING FOR HELP

Away from the main roads you have no alternative but to use a mobile to call for help, but first, gather information. If you are in a town, find out what street you are on. If you are out of town, try to remember the last village or town you went through. Some mobile phone traffic information services start with phrases like 'You are on the A11 near Thetford ...' and if your phone has internet connection it may give access to a mapping website that recognizes where you are.

Many sat navs have a 'find me' or 'help me' facility which instantly gives your location, including the name of the road, nearest town and a GPS position which is particularly useful in guiding air ambulances to accidents in remote locations. Check whether yours has it.

As on the motorway, you need your breakdown organization membership number, car make, model and registration number but you also need the breakdown organization's phone number, which you should programme into your phone and have written down in case of problems with the phone.

Personal safety

Apart from the dangers from other traffic, being stranded at the roadside leaves you vulnerable in other ways though the majority of people who stop are likely to be doing nothing more sinister than offering help.

If you are or feel vulnerable, make sure the motorway controller or your breakdown organization know. If waiting by the car, leave the passenger door ajar so you can jump in and lock it if necessary. Talk to people through a partially open window until you are sure they are genuine and don't accept lifts from strangers unless you absolutely have to. If you do, make a note, perhaps on your mobile phone, of the car's registration number.

Breakdown organizations sometimes use contract garages instead of their patrols. These people should know who you are and have details of the incident. If they can't provide proof that the organization sent them, call your breakdown service provider and check. It could be a garage trying to trick you into letting them work on the car to surprise you with a bill later, claiming you asked them to do it, or even someone with more dangerous intentions.

Changing a wheel

A puncture is the most likely 'breakdown', not least because it is something that afflicts all cars regardless of how new or well maintained they are.

> **WARNING!** ⚠
>
> To change a wheel you must be on firm, fairly level ground or the jack may slip at the wrong moment.

The wheel-changing mistake most people make is to start jacking it up first, so let's start at the beginning.

1 *If you don't know where the car's **jacking points** are, check the handbook. These are areas of the body that have been shaped or reinforced to take the jack and the stresses of lifting the car.*
2 *Now, apply the handbrake and put a manual gearbox in gear or an automatic in park to eliminate the risk of it rolling.*

Top tip

Using the gearbox to help hold it steady is especially important when lifting one of the wheels on which the handbrake works, which is usually at the back, although a few front-wheel drive cars have handbrakes on the front, notably older Saabs and Citroëns.

3 *Get the tools and spare wheel out and if your car has alloy wheels with locking wheel nuts, you'll need the key if it is not kept with the wheel brace.*
4 *Remove the wheel trim, if it has one. There may be a special hook tool for this in the toolkit. With locking wheel nuts there is often a chromed cap that is removed with a tool that looks like a plastic socket spanner.*
5 *Now use the wheel brace to loosen all the nuts so they are finger tight. By doing this before you jack the car up, you can exert force without fear of rocking the car off the jack or*

*having the wheel turn instead of the nut. Wheel nuts usually
undo anti-clockwise.*

6 *Now jack the car up, making sure that the jack isn't slipping
as the car's weight is taken up.*

Top tip

Raise the wheel more than is needed to remove the flat tyre
because the inflated one is taller.

7 *Completely remove the wheel nuts, putting them somewhere
safe and clean, like onto the tool pouch or an upturned
wheel-trim.*
8 *Lift the wheel off, remembering it will be dirty and heavy,
especially if it is a steel wheel.*
9 *Lift the spare wheel onto the hub aligning the holes in the
wheel with the threaded studs or holes in the hub. Hold the
wheel against the hub with your hand or foot and put the nuts
on finger tight.*
10 *Lower the wheel to the ground and fully tighten the nuts in
diagonal pairs to evenly pull the wheel onto the hub. Do not
apply excessive force or you may damage the threads or even
stretch the studs that the nuts screw onto.*

Top tip

Most people finish off by going once round the nuts in order,
checking their tightness because a nut can feel tight until
its diagonally opposite number pulls the wheel on flat. You
should recheck the nuts for tightness after about 30 miles.

11 *Replace any wheel-trims then properly stow tools and the
wheel you removed. If you have a pressure gauge, check the
spare's tyre pressure or do it at a garage soon afterwards,
unless you have checked it recently.*

STICKING WHEELS

A wheel can get stuck to the hub by corrosion. Sometimes it is
enough to lever it with the wheel brace, though don't lever against
the shiny brake disc or you may scar the disc badly enough for it to

need replacing. Also remember that alloy wheels are softer than the steel brace so can be damaged by it.

If leverage isn't possible or doesn't work, try putting the wheel nuts back on so they are not quite touching the wheel, then lower it back to the ground. Often the car's weight is enough to loosen it. If not you can try levering or rocking it, but if this fails you need help from your breakdown organization.

Alternative spares

As explained in Chapter 6, some cars are supplied with a space-saver spare tyre, temporary repair kit or runflat tyres.

Figure 10.1 Tighten wheel nuts in diagonal pairs to pull wheel evenly onto the hub.

SPACE SAVERS

If it is a space saver, it has a speed limit, usually of 50 mph, which is often displayed as a sticker on the wheel and is certainly in the handbook, along with any mileage limit (see Plate 9). Note that the wheel stickers often show the limit as kilometres per hour (kph). It is illegal to exceed the limit and the wheels are now painted a bright colour so the police can see you have a space saver in use.

REPAIR KITS

Temporary repair kits are either a canister of sealant mixed with compressed air to repair and reinflate in one go or, more commonly now, a sealant and an electric tyre pump (see Plate 10). Follow the instructions for their use in the handbook and get the tyre properly repaired as soon as possible. However, if the tyre has a large hole, do not waste the kit trying to seal it, call your breakdown organization instead.

RUNFLATS

Runflat tyres also have a speed and distance limit, given in the handbook. Though you can carry on driving, it is sensible, when safe, to check it to make sure the tyre isn't so severely damaged there is a risk of it breaking up and that it doesn't have any large objects stuck in it that might come flying out or damage the wheel rim.

The wrong fuel

Thousands of motorists a year put the wrong fuel into their cars. These days it is usually diesel car drivers filling with petrol, because diesel fuel nozzles are larger than those for unleaded petrol, but if you have an old non-catalyst petrol car it is possible to fill it with diesel because it has a larger filler pipe.

If you know you've done it, don't try to start the car because it will mean having to clean the entire fuel system instead of just the tank and may do serious damage. A petrol car won't run for long with diesel in the system, anyway.

DIESEL DANGER

The most serious damage you can do is to run a modern diesel with any amount of petrol in the system. It was said to be safe to run old diesels with a small amount of petrol contaminating the fuel, though you had to be sure it was a small amount. Modern direct injection and common rail diesels have fuel systems powered by high speed electronic pumps that run at extremely high pressures (20,000 to 30,000 psi) and they need the lubricating properties of the diesel oil to do it. Petrol dilutes the oil, robbing it of its lubricating qualities.

So, if you run a modern diesel on petrol-contaminated fuel you will almost certainly need a new pump and, probably, new injectors, which is a hefty repair bill your insurers will refuse to cover unless the service station made a mistake.

If you make the mistake, call your breakdown organization or a garage to get the car towed in so the system can be cleaned.

A touch of glass

The days of windscreens that shattered into a lace of glass cubes are passing, thankfully, though side windows still do it.

There are two main types of glass used in cars: toughened and laminated. Toughened can take a lot of knocks but when it breaks, stress patterns in the glass make it break into small cubes, which, though sharp, are not as dangerous as shards would be. Laminated glass is two layers of glass, the inner one of which may also be toughened, sandwiching a plastic membrane which spreads stress and holds the glass together if it is broken.

LAMINATED GLASS

It has long been a requirement for new cars to have laminated windscreens because they are safer. It is less likely that anything hitting the screen will come into the car and if an unbelted occupant is thrown into the screen it usually bends enough to absorb some of the impact but keeps them in the car. A few cars are now fitted with laminated side windows, or offered with it as an option, because of its anti-theft and sound deadening properties, but most still have toughened glass in windows other than the windscreen.

CHIP REPAIRS

Where a stone thrown up by another vehicle would shatter toughened screens, a laminated screen is more likely to chip, if it is damaged at all. Don't ignore these chips because they can weaken the glass and allow water to seep between the layers. If repaired quickly it can save having to replace the whole windscreen.

Chips are repaired by pumping transparent resin in under pressure. There are DIY kits that claim to do the same, but one wonders how they can effect a sound repair when they do not work under pressure. A professional repair of this sort is very cheap, especially when compared with the cost of a replacement screen, which is why insurance companies are often prepared to pay for them even though they are much less than the policy's excess.

However, not all chips are repairable. If they are too large or cracks are starting to run out from them, they can't be fixed. If they are in the driver's line of sight they are not usually repaired because they can still be seen and a car will not usually pass an MOT test if there are visible marks in that area.

Unfortunately, even if chips are repaired, the stress they cause can start a crack which gradually creeps up the glass. If this happens, the windscreen must be replaced as soon as possible. In modern cars the glass is bonded to the body and often contributes significantly to the overall strength of the bodyshell so a crack weakens it. That's not to say that a small crack makes the car dangerous, but a small crack will grow.

TOUGHENED GLASS

If a toughened glass windscreen shatters it has an area in front of the driver that breaks into larger pieces so you can still see through well enough to get to safety. With any toughened glass pane there is a chance that a second impact will make it burst into the car, so don't be tempted to drive with it in place. However, don't try punching it out, as suggested in films, because you can seriously injure yourself. If you need to remove the glass, do so wearing gloves or with hands wrapped in cloth.

Insight

If a toughened glass window breaks it covers you in tiny splinters of glass, so don't brush your clothes with your bare hands. Close your eyes if you have to pull clothes over your head because the material is full of splinters that might harm them. You might even have to throw clothes away, especially knitted garments, because the glass splinters won't wash out. As soon as you can, brush or comb your hair, no matter how little you have, with your eyes closed and head tilted forwards, then wash it thoroughly.

DRIVING WINDOWLESS

If you lose a windscreen and need to drive the car you must keep your speed down or the air pressure inside the car may pop out other windows. If the rear screen goes, drive with a front window open to prevent exhaust fumes being sucked back into the car.

Getting repairs

If you have a common car, a glass repair specialist may be able to replace a broken screen or side window quickly enough to get you on your way but if they can't, you'll have to make a temporary repair with plastic and tape, but remove broken glass first. If you must park a car with a broken window, take everything of value out of it.

If you have comprehensive insurance it almost certainly has glass cover for a limited number of replacements a year. Often resin repairs don't count towards that limit, so the insurer might pay for several of those but only one windscreen replacement. Some insurers have cost limits on glass cover if it is not by their preferred supplier, so check before you book a repair. Many repairers now deal direct with the insurance companies, saving you the bother, but they need your policy details.

Smash and grab

Glass is the weak point in modern cars' security so avoid tempting smash and grab opportunists. Never leave valuables on display or anything that suggests valuables, like sat nav mounting brackets, CD cases or bags (even empty ones).

If glass breakage was criminal, your insurer will require you to report it to the police and get an incident or crime number.

Mechanical breakdown

WARNING! ⚠

If mechanical breakdown involves the steering, brakes, clutch or gearbox giving up, there is little you can do at the roadside except call for help. It is very dangerous to carry on driving with faults to the braking or steering systems.

RUNNING ON EMPTY

If the engine misbehaves, you may be able to do something. If it gently runs out of power, perhaps stuttering as it does so, it is likely to be a fuel problem.

Check the fuel gauge but even if that registers fuel, think about when you last filled up. If the car seems to have been unusually economical, you may have a faulty gauge. If you are in a quiet place, try taking the fuel filler cap off and rocking the car to see if you can hear fuel sloshing about. If you can't then you have probably run out.

If you decide to get more, rather than calling out the breakdown organization, make sure you get it in a canister designed to carry the fuel, which should come with a flexible nozzle so you can pour it into the tank without spillage. It is illegal to transport petrol in any other type of container because it is explosively flammable and as it warms up gives off vapour which can burst inadequate containers.

ENGINE ELECTRICS

If an engine suddenly stops, it is more likely to be an electrical problem. Before you call for help, just check connections. With the ignition off, give sparkplug leads a push onto the plug and follow them through to make sure connectors at the other end are on. On older cars with a conventional **distributor** instead of modern electronic ignition, a common fault is that a thin lead running to the distributor, called the low tension lead, comes undone or breaks. The distributor is the bit all the leads go to, like a plastic octopus.

SPLASH!

If a sudden stop happens after hitting water, you may have splashed water over the ignition leads. If the leads are old, the water seeps into invisible cracks in the insulation and shorts them out. With the ignition off, try drying all the leads, connections and distributor cap with a cloth or tissues and seeing if the car will restart. However, if this happens with a diesel, don't try to restart it because diesels don't have an ignition to get wet, so if it has stopped you have almost certainly forced water into the engine air intake and starting it could cause serious damage as the engine tries to compress water instead of gas. You need professional help.

ELECTRICAL FAILURES

If electrical items fail with the engine still running, turn the ignition off and check the fuses. With lights, a single one going out is probably bulb failure but if more than one goes out it could be the fuse or a wiring fault, though a fuse usually works the front and rear sidelights on one side rather than both fronts or both backs.

A headlight with bulb failure usually works on beam but not dip, or vice versa, and a combined brake/tail light works as one but not the other, but if both functions fail, check the fuse before replacing the bulb.

Top tip
If all the lights go out, check that the earth strap is still connected: it is either a cable or a braided metal strap from the battery's negative connection to the body.

CHANGING FUSES

The handbook tells you where the fuses are and which fuses work what, which may also be printed or moulded into the fusebox lid.

Fuses sometimes blow because of a very temporary problem and sometimes seem to go just because they're old, but if they repeatedly blow, there is a fault that should be investigated professionally. Modern fuses are easy to check because they have a hole in the plastic through which you can see if the fuse strip is still intact. Most fuse boxes have a little pair of tweezers for removing and replacing fuses (see Plate 14).

The fuses are colour coded and numbered according to amperage. You must replace a fuse with one of the same amperage because a lower amperage will blow straight away and a higher one does not protect the wiring. If it has a 10 amp fuse it's because the wiring is designed for 10 amp – fitting a 20 or 30 amp fuse means the power could exceed the wires' capacity which is a fire risk.

> **Top tip**
> If you do not have a fuse of the right amperage for something vital in the car, look at what else fuses of that amperage run. You can do without interior lights to run the indicators, or sacrifice the heated rear screen for the wipers.

Starting problems

Before you get into a panic when the car won't start, make sure it is a fault. Read the 'Starting' section in Chapter 4, or in the handbook, to make sure you are not being thwarted by safety or security devices, or your own mistakes.

STEP BY STEP

Having established that you aren't doing something stupid, start looking for problems.

1 *If it is turning over normally are you sure it has fuel? See 'Running on empty' earlier in this chapter.*
2 *Check the battery connections are tight.*
3 *If it is not turning over at all, do the lights work?*
   ▷ *No: the battery is totally flat. If so, jump-starting is the only way of getting it going other than taking the battery out and giving it several hours on a charger. Indeed, if it is this flat it may need a heftier kick of power than most ordinary car batteries can supply, so you need to call out your breakdown service even if jump-leads are available to you. (Safe jump-starting is covered further on.)*
   ▷ *Yes: look under the bonnet and check that there are no obviously damaged wires or connections to the ignition or starter motor. Most cables associated with starting are thick ones.*

4 *The engine turns over but the lights dim: the battery power is weak and a jump-start should help.*

5 *The engine turns over but lights stay bright: either fuel isn't getting through or power isn't.*

▷ *If it is a fuel-feed problem, especially in very hot weather when fuel can vaporize in the pipes, trying again later might help. With old carburettor cars it is also possible, by incorrect starting, to flood the engine with too much petrol, which you can always smell, and all you can do is leave it for 20 minutes to evaporate.*

▷ *Power problems on older cars are common on damp days because the moisture shorts the power away through minute cracks in the cable insulation. If it is doing this you can often see it in the dark or in the shade of a barely lifted bonnet. Drying the cables may get it started. Spraying with WD40 can also repel the water. You can buy spray sealants to prevent it happening again, though new cables are the best long-term solution if this frequently happens. If the car has a distributor, moisture gets inside the cap if it is cracked, so dry inside that and replace it with a new one as soon as you can.*

MODERN SYSTEMS

Modern cars are much less prone to these types of starting problems with their electronic ignitions and fuel systems, but if they do suffer an electrical starting problem there is little you can do about it. Fortunately, modern electronic diagnostic equipment should make tracing the problem easier for the garage than hunting out poor connections and cracked cable insulation on old cars.

Push-starting

There are few cars on the road today you can safely push start. It can seriously damage automatic gearboxes and is not recommended for cars with catalytic converters because if it pumps unburned petrol into the exhaust it can damage the converter, especially if it ignites when the engine starts. Any petrol car built after 1990 may have a catalytic converter and all modern ones do: if it has a narrow fuel filler pipe it almost certainly has a 'cat'. Push-starting diesels is not advisable because firstly, they can be very hard to push and secondly, if unburned fuel gathers in the **cylinders** the pistons can become hydraulic rams trying to lift the roof of the combustion chamber.

So if you have an old, manual, petrol car and energetic friends, you can try push-starting. You need a good stretch of flat or downhill road. Put the car in second or third gear and, with the ignition on, handbrake off and clutch pedal down, get the friends to start pushing. When you get a decent speed up, bring the clutch up and hope it starts. It is safest if one of the pushers is nominated to shout 'now' to say when the clutch is let in so they are not surprised by the car jolting or suddenly driving away.

Top tip

Until the engine starts you have no assistance to the steering or brakes so it will take more effort to work them. Don't be tempted to try tow-starting because when the sick car starts there is a strong risk of it hitting the tow-car.

Jump-starting

WARNING! ⚠

Batteries are dangerous. The power is direct current so if your body or tools make a connection between live and neutral terminals (which includes the car's bodywork) the current holds you instead of jolting you away like the alternating current in your house would. That is always painful and can cause serious burns. It can damage the car, too. Never try to jump-start a damaged battery or it might burst, spraying acid.

Modern cars have many electronic systems that won't take kindly to a power surge so it is vital to check the car's handbook in case there are any precautions you must take before jump-starting. Indeed, if your handbook's advice differs from that given here, follow its instructions because the manufacturer must have a good reason for it and if you cause damage by doing anything else it isn't covered by the warranty.

You must use jump-leads specifically designed for the job and that are in good condition with no damage to the insulation – if it makes contact with something it shouldn't, including your hands, it could do serious damage. When buying jump-leads look for the **DIN** approval number 72 553 which shows they are of a safe standard.

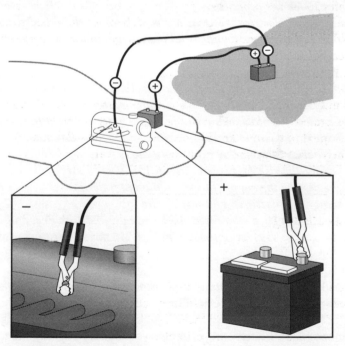

Figure 10.2 Jump-start cables both go to the dead battery but the negative one is clipped to bare metal on the donor car.

Both batteries must be of the same voltage: you can't start a 12 volt car with a 24 volt lorry, for example. Some large diesel engines, like those in off-roaders, may need a more substantial boost of power than small car batteries can manage, even though both are 12 volt. We will assume both cars have a negative earth, which means a cable from the battery's negative terminal goes direct to the car's body. Vehicles with a positive earth tend to be classic cars.

▶ *The negative terminal is identified with a minus sign (–) and sometimes colour coded black. The positive one has a plus sign (+) and may be picked out with red.*

1 *The cars need to be close together but must not touch. Take care when opening doors during jump-starting that they do not touch the other car.*
2 *Check all electrical systems are switched off, though if you are on or near the road you should leave the donor car's hazard lights on.*
3 *With both ignitions off, connect the red jump lead to the positive terminal on the flat battery then connect the other end to the positive terminal on the donor battery.*
4 *Connect the black cable to the negative terminal on the donor battery. The other end is not connected to the flat battery but to that car's engine or bodywork away from the battery, to reduce the risk of a short circuit. It is best to attach it to bare metal, like the engine block. In many modern cars the front wings are plastic so will not do the job.*
5 *Check you have connected the terminals, like with like, and that the cables are clear of the engine fan and the exhaust manifold.*

Top tip
The latest advice is to wait a few minutes to allow the voltages between the two cars to stabilize.

6 *Start the donor car and bring it to a fast idle, then try starting the car with the flat battery. Do not run its starter for more than 15 seconds at a time and if the jump leads become hot, stop to allow them to cool.*

Top tip

If the car with the flat battery still won't start you may have another problem. Most likely, you need a new battery because the lead plates inside have collapsed so you no longer have a connection running through it (see Chapter 7).

7 *When you remove the cables, do it in the reverse order, disconnecting the black lead first then the red. This reduces the risk of sparking by disconnecting the earth first.*

Modern methods

With some cars the handbook may advise running the donor car with the batteries connected for 15 minutes to charge the flat battery, then disconnecting everything before starting the car with the flat battery. This is to protect the car's electronics.

Professional help

If a car regularly suffers a flat battery check there is nothing draining it, like an interior light staying on, then get the battery and charging system checked professionally.

10 THINGS TO REMEMBER

1 *Join a breakdown organization.*

2 *Make sure you know where the car's tools and spare wheel live.*

3 *Keep a high visibility vest in the car.*

4 *In the event of something going wrong safety must be your first priority.*

5 *Motorway hard shoulders are dangerous so use hazard lights and keep an eye on the traffic.*

6 *Use motorway emergency phones to tell the authorities you are there even if you have a mobile or can deal with the problem yourself.*

7 *Take care when rejoining a motorway and build up speed on the hard shoulder.*

8 *Loosen wheel nuts BEFORE jacking up the car.*

9 *Tighten wheel nuts in diagonal pairs.*

10 *Never start a modern diesel if you have put petrol in by mistake.*

11

Accidents

In this chapter you will learn:
- **what to do at the scene of an accident**
- **how to make an insurance claim**
- **how to get your car repaired.**

If you manage to go through your driving career without being involved in an accident you will be very lucky. Fortunately, the majority of accidents are damage only, but even one where only the cars get hurt can be traumatic, particularly as modern cars protect occupants so well that they can still involve very severe impacts.

Top tip

> As we said in Chapter 10 on Breakdowns, it is wise to carry a first aid kit, warning triangle, fire extinguisher and high visibility vest. In some countries many, if not all, these items are compulsory. Stow them safely and where you can get them quickly.

If you are involved in an accident keep your temper and don't panic. Whatever you do, don't leap out of the car to confront the other driver, but assess the situation first. You could easily leap into the path of another vehicle whose driver is too busy gawping at the accident to notice you. So, check passengers are all right and see what is happening on the road around you.

It is only in films that all crashed cars immediately explode into flames. In real life that is extremely rare and even then the car must be so severely damaged that fuel tank protection and fuel shut-off systems have been wrecked. Diesel cars are safer still because the fuel needs to get so hot to ignite.

However, it is still unwise to smoke after an accident and, especially if you smell petrol, you should walk away from the wreckage before using a mobile phone. The signal from a mobile can cause sparks off metalwork in certain circumstances, which is why you are not allowed to use them in filling stations.

Insight

One of the odd things about the scene of an accident is how people wander around waiting for someone to do something. Avoid being bossy, but if you just calmly start asking people to do things, order will start to appear from chaos. Make sure you assign jobs to individuals, like calling the emergency services, staying with the injured or directing traffic. If you say 'will someone call an ambulance' the chances are nobody will, but if you tell an individual to do it they will get on with it. Even in a minor accident, people often need someone to say to them 'let's get the cars out of the road and exchange details'.

Legal requirements

Legal requirements at the scenes of accidents vary from state to state, so check locally. There are few, if any, countries in which you are not legally obliged to stop after an accident no matter how minor. In the UK you must give your name and address and that of the vehicle's owner to anyone having reasonable grounds to ask for it.

NON-INJURY ACCIDENTS

If it is a damage-only accident and you don't give your name and address to the owner of the damaged property at the time, you must report it to the police within 24 hours. This doesn't just apply if you damage another car, but if you damage anything, including fences, road signs and telegraph poles as well as most domesticated animals.

INJURY ACCIDENTS

If anyone is hurt, you must report the accident to the police within 24 hours, regardless of whether you exchanged details at the scene, and produce your insurance certificate within seven days. If you don't have the certificate or your driving licence for administrative reasons, tell the police within seven days so they can give you an extension until it arrives.

GETTING HELP

Some people think the police must be called to all accidents and vehicles can't be moved until they have arrived. This is not so in the UK and failure to move vehicles only holds everyone else up, though you should not move vehicles with injured people in them. If a damage-only accident blocks the road, or part of it, because the cars are so severely damaged they can't be moved, you may have to call the police to safely direct traffic and help arrange recovery. Some insurers and breakdown organizations have accident helplines where they can arrange recovery of a badly-damaged car as well as giving you advice on what to do.

At the scene

WARNING! ⚠

No matter how badly damaged the car is, or whose fault it is, the first priority must be to any casualties and to ensuring road safety at the scene. Always ensure you do not become a casualty while helping others or just by being there. Ensure nobody else is going to crash into your crash, getting someone to direct the traffic if necessary and always keeping an eye on oncoming vehicles yourself.

CASUALTIES

We can't go into roadside first aid in detail here. At least read a book like the Red Cross approved *Five-Minute First Aid for Travel* published by Hodder Education or, better still, take a first aid course. If there are casualties call for expert help by dialling the emergency services before you try to do anything else and if you ask someone else to make the call, tell them to let you know when it has been made successfully so you can be sure it has been done. Unless you are a trained first aider you should stick to ensuring people can breathe and are in as little danger as possible.

> **Top tip**
> When checking casualties, start with the unconscious and quiet ones – if they can scream they can breathe.

Do not move serious casualties unless they are in danger. Be particularly careful where neck and back injuries are suspected because moving someone with damage to the vertebrae could turn them from a casualty with a treatable injury into a paraplegic for the rest of their life. Neck injuries are very common in motorcyclists and horse riders and to car occupants, as a result of whiplash, when a car has been struck from behind. Helmets and safety hats should never be removed from casualties because of the risk of worsening head and neck injuries.

Bleeding can be slowed down by applying pressure, taking care not to move broken bones or push debris into the wound. If someone has an object stuck in them, do not try to extract it because pulling it out may do further damage, perhaps to a blood vessel or vital organ.

RECORDING THE SCENE

When casualties have been taken care of, or in non-injury accidents, take a note and, if you can, photos, of the position of the vehicles and move them out of the road if possible.

Swap details with the other drivers, asking to see their driving licence or other identification to confirm who they are. In addition to the information you are legally required to give it also makes sense to give them a phone number and your insurer's name and address, with your insurance policy number. Keep a note of these things in the car.

Also make sure you get the registration numbers, makes, models and colours of the other cars involved as well as details of what damage you can see, so nobody can claim for a different car or damage you didn't do.

Note down:

- ▶ *the time of the accident*
- ▶ *your speed when it happened*
- ▶ *the weather and road conditions (was it wet, dry, icy or covered in loose chippings)*
- ▶ *what lights vehicles were showing, including your own*
- ▶ *the name of the road and the names of roads at any nearby junctions (you may have to check this on a map later if name signs are not visible)*
- ▶ *speed limit signs especially if it is different to the national limit for the road (like 50 mph on a rural dual carriageway where the limit is normally 70 mph).*

Make a sketch map of the scene showing the positions of the cars, witnesses, road markings and signs.

Top tip

Some insurers include a pamphlet with their paperwork to help you record details at the scene, so keep that in the car, too.

LIABILITY

Do not admit liability. That means you do not say it was your fault even if it was and do not say things like 'I'm sorry, I didn't see you'. There are two reasons for this: firstly, you are probably not a legal expert and even if you were, you would not be in a state to thoroughly assess the situation; and secondly, your insurance policy expressly forbids you to admit liability – that's what you pay your insurer to sort out. If anyone pressurizes you, simply point out that all insurance policies have this clause and if anyone involved in the accident breaks that condition it could make it harder to get payments sorted out. This is not strictly true because the insurers would probably pay for repairs and other compensation, then argue over who was really to blame and who's going to foot the bill, so take note if anyone else admits liability.

WITNESSES

If there are any witnesses, for either side, take their names and addresses and a note of where they were when they saw what happened. If anyone is reluctant to get involved, point out that next time they could be the person in your situation and that the most onerous thing they are likely to have to do is fill in a short form saying what they have seen. If someone refuses, especially in an injury accident, take their car number so they can be traced if things get difficult or if the police want to get them to a court or inquest.

Leaving the scene

Before driving off, assess the condition of your car.

- ▶ *Is it safe and legal?*
- ▶ *Is it leaking anything?*
- ▶ *Do the lights work?*
- ▶ *Are the tyres damaged?*
- ▶ *Do the doors close properly?*
- ▶ *Is there any broken glass that needs removing?*
- ▶ *Does it still have number plates?*

AT THE WHEEL

When you start driving, does it feel right? Apply the brakes to check they work at low speed before going any faster. If you have any doubts about these things, arrange recovery.

If you are comprehensively insured, recovery will be covered by the insurer, though the policy may insist you arrange it through their accident helpline. If you only have third party cover, you may be able to get it back off the other driver's policy, if they are to blame (we'll look at recovering uninsured loss later).

Any car in which the airbags have gone off is likely to be too badly damaged to drive because the bags only go off in severe impacts.

If you drive off and have another accident when something fails, you will be entirely to blame and the car may not be able to give you full crash protection.

ARE YOU ALL RIGHT?

Remember, you are shaken up, so drive cautiously and always stop and look carefully in both directions at junctions. When you are under such stress, your brain does not react quickly enough to register moving objects if your head is also moving as you look for them.

Don't drive if you feel odd, especially if you have hit your head and don't be surprised if about 15 minutes after the accident you suddenly feel dreadful, even shaking or crying. This is the effect of coming down from the adrenaline rush the accident provoked and you must at least stop until you feel better. The best thing is to get someone to collect you, go home on public transport or book into a hotel. After a serious accident you may also stiffen up, but go to a doctor if you have serious problems moving or any strange sensations.

After the accident

You must tell your insurer as soon as possible after an accident, even if it is so minor you don't think there will be a claim. If it turns out later that one of the cars involved was more badly damaged than at first appeared or someone was more seriously hurt, a claim might result against you and the insurer could get difficult if you haven't reported it. If there is no claim, make sure before the policy is renewed that they do not still have it on their books as unresolved or they might increase your premium.

AIDE MEMOIR

It is a good idea to write down what happened as soon as you can so you don't forget details and can be sure you have all the information you need, like road names. Also, this helps you to get what you are going to say sorted out if your insurer is one who takes details over the phone. Insurers who do this usually send you the completed form to be signed and for you to add your map of the scene and photos to. If they do this, read it carefully to make sure it says everything you told them and add any details you have remembered since. Check your policy to make sure you have done all you should and to see what you are entitled to.

THIRD PARTY CONTACT

You may be contacted by other people's insurers. Any communication from them should go direct to your insurer. If you wish you can let them know you have passed it on, but say nothing else – all communication now, between you and those involved in the accident, or their representatives, should be through your insurer. They are (or should be) the experts in dealing with such matters and you have been paying them to provide this help. Also tell them if the police take action.

YOUR CHOICE

Some insurers claim to look after everything for you, but there will inevitably be some work for you to do because their repairers still need to see the car to see what must be done. Some will come to you, others may insist you go to them, but see what your insurer says you are entitled to and complain if you are not getting it.

Insurers want you to use their preferred repairer but you don't have to if this doesn't suit you. If you don't you may lose the rights to things like a courtesy car while yours is repaired but you must weigh up the pros and cons:

▶ *Is it worth it if you have got to go miles out of your way for estimates and to take your car in?*
▶ *Most preferred repairer's work is warranted for a year, but your car's perforation (rust) warranty may be several times that and depend on repairs being done to the manufacturer's standards.*

▶ *If you have a specialist car, say, something with an aluminium or composite body, can you be sure the preferred repairer has the necessary skills? Indeed, with such cars the preferred repairer may subcontract the work to the local franchised dealer for the marque, so you may as well deal direct.*

ARRANGING REPAIRS YOURSELF

If you decide to go it alone, your insurer will want an estimate from your repairer and may insist you pay the difference if it is a lot more than their repairer would have wanted. But that is unlikely because most repairers use a computerized estimate system developed by the insurance industry. However, if you are paying for the repair yourself, perhaps because you only have third party insurance or the damage costs less than your excess to put right, get more than one quote because it may save you money.

Whoever does the repairs, check what they are replacing, what they are repairing and that they are using new parts, preferably the manufacturer's own, not ones salvaged from other vehicles, unless it is an old car.

COMPLETION

When the work is done, don't sign any paperwork without checking the car. A properly carried out repair should not be visible, especially not on a fairly new car. On a very old car where the paint has lost its shine it may be impossible to get a complete match between new and old, but otherwise the paintwork should match in both colour and finish. There should certainly be no overspray on trim or door and window seals. If you are not happy with it, don't sign the paperwork and tell your insurer.

Modern paints are fast drying and often baked to harden them, but the new paint should still be treated carefully because it will be easier to mark until it has hardened off completely. Certainly don't rush home and polish the car because the slightly abrasive effect of the polish may damage the surface of the new paint.

Write-offs

A write-off is a car that is so badly damaged that the cost of repair is greater than the value of the car, so the insurer writes it off the books as a loss. Sometimes the car may not look that badly damaged to an inexpert eye, but a careful inspection, sometimes with highly accurate body measuring equipment, may have revealed hidden damage to the basic structure. With high value cars they may put it on a jig to straighten it out, but with most cars it is not worth it and many people say cars damaged to this extent never feel right afterwards. In addition, the forces involved in a crash can behave in unexpected ways, causing damage where you would never guess to look.

Insight

I was once shown a Land Rover Defender that had been written off after a low speed head-on crash. Damage to the front of the car appeared relatively minor, but when it was put on a ramp you could see extensive damage to the rear suspension and chassis. That was because the force of the impact had travelled up the chassis rails on each side and met at the back of the car where it hit crossmembers and the suspension like a giant hammer blow. This is a characteristic of many vehicles with a separate chassis and meant it could not be economically repaired.

The insurer pays you the market value of a written-off car, unless it is covered by GAP insurance which gives replacement value (see Chapter 1). Unfortunately, market value is less than you paid for it unless you bought it very recently, which can be a problem if you are buying it on finance.

QUERYING THE OFFER

If you think the insurer's offer is excessively low, use an online car valuation service like Glass's (www.glass.co.uk) to get a value for the car and see if the offer is fair. If not, complain and if they do not improve the offer, seek independent advice from your motoring organization. Some people say it pays to complain regardless of how good the first offer proves.

All insurance policies lay down a disputes procedure in the policy document. If the accident wasn't your fault you may be able to claim any losses as a result of write-off from the other person's insurers as uninsured losses, explained further on.

Once you have been paid, the car belongs to the insurer and you must hand over the registration document and inform the DVLA that you have done so. The car will then be listed as a write-off, which is graded from those that are repairable at a cost through to those that can only be scrapped.

Other claims

Don't forget that your insurance is not only there to pay for repairs to cars. It also covers death and injuries and, if it is comprehensive, it may have cover for belongings, hire cars, legal assistance and loss of earnings. Some of this cover may only be for third parties, including passengers, but if an accident costs you money in some way other than damage to the car, it is worth looking at what you can claim.

But never make a false claim because if you are caught out it is treated as fraud and may make it hard or expensive to get insurance in the future.

CAR CRIME

If a claim is as a result of car crime, you must report it to the police first, no matter how minor. They give you a crime or incident number which your insurer needs as proof that you have reported it. In most cases that is all you can expect from the police.

In the event of theft of the car, or anything stolen from it, the insurer waits for a period laid down in the policy before paying, in case the property is recovered. If the car is not recovered, the situation is like that with write-offs, described earlier. If this leaves you without a car, or lacking items you need for work, check whether your policy covers hiring these things while you wait.

With property, most policies have limits on the value of items covered. You may find property is covered by household policies. There are usually restrictions on items left in unattended cars, especially high value things like cameras and laptops.

If a stolen car or property is recovered after you have been paid, it belongs to the insurer but you can buy back recovered items, for example, those of sentimental value.

Police may refer you to victim support groups who can explain if you are entitled to compensation from official bodies for uninsured losses. In the UK, the Citizens' Advice Bureau may also advise on this.

Uninsured losses

There may be costs associated with an accident that are not covered by your insurance but that doesn't mean you have to pay if it wasn't your fault. These might include:

- ▶ *all your own repairs if you only had third party insurance*
- ▶ *the excess on any policy*
- ▶ *loss of earnings*
- ▶ *costs of replacing the car or paying off finance beyond the write-off payment*
- ▶ *the cost of hiring a car while yours was repaired*
- ▶ *repair or replacement of uninsured property in the car.*

Your own insurer might be willing to advise whether making an uninsured loss claim against the other driver or their insurance is valid.

MAKING A CLAIM

If you are reasonable, and lucky, you might get paid with nothing more than a polite letter to the other person or their insurer. Some progressive insurers, when they know their client is to blame, call the third party to offer help, like a courtesy car. The thinking is that if you see how thoughtful they are you might come to them next time you renew your insurance.

However, not all insurers and their clients are so helpful and you may have to argue. Some comprehensive policies include legal assistance for this sort of action and motoring organizations might also help. There are even a couple of used-car warranties that include legal assistance and your trade union or professional body may act for you, especially if the accident happened while you were working. If not, seek advice from your local Citizens' Advice Bureau or a lawyer or take action in a small claims court, which is the County Court in England and Wales and Sheriff's Court in Scotland. Your local court can supply advice pamphlets or the information is on the Trading Standards national website at www.tradingstandards.gov.uk.

CLAIMS AGAINST YOU

If another driver writes to you claiming uninsured losses, pass the letter on to your insurer. To stop the other person bothering you, let them know you have passed the letter on and suggest future correspondence be addressed direct to your insurer to speed things up.

However, sometimes the first you know of someone pursuing uninsured losses is when their lawyers write to you threatening legal action claiming previous approaches have been unsuccessful. This means they have been chasing your insurer without success. If this happens let them know you are taking it up with your insurer, without commenting on the situation, then send their letter to your insurer with a strongly worded letter complaining about the way they have handled it and the distress caused to you by threatened court action.

You paid premiums to cover your costs and reduce the hassle of an accident and if they have been so tardy in handling claims against you that lawyers are now hassling you personally, they haven't been doing what you paid for.

10 THINGS TO REMEMBER

1 *After an accident keep calm, keep your temper and assess the situation before leaping out into the road.*

2 *You are required by law to stop after an accident and give your details and those of the car and its owner to anyone with reasonable grounds to ask for them.*

3 *All injury accidents and damage-only accidents where you were unable to give your details to the property owner must be reported to the police within 24 hours.*

4 *Safety and the wellbeing of casualties must take priority over everything else at an accident scene.*

5 *Call emergency services before trying to help casualties.*

6 *Only move casualties if they are in danger.*

7 *Take notes at the scene of information your insurers require, draw a road plan and take pictures if possible.*

8 *Do not admit liability but take note if anyone else does.*

9 *Check your car before leaving the scene and do not drive if you feel odd.*

10 *Make sure you are aware of everything you can claim for from your own and others' insurance, but do not lie to insurers.*

12

....

Selling the car

In this chapter you will learn:
- *how to prepare your car to sell it*
- *about trade-ins vs private sale*
- *how to advertise and sell a car.*

No matter how much you like your car, there comes a day
when you want to change it. Don't fool yourself that keeping
a car running is cheaper than buying a newer one. There is a
point where the cost of keeping an ageing car on the road is
more than the cost of buying a newer one. Indeed, if you buy
a new car, you can be fairly sure annual motoring costs will
become more predictable because it is unlikely to need expensive
repairs.

If you bought your car new, or fairly new, you must think of
the money you are losing through depreciation. If you keep
it much beyond three years your losses over the life of the car
are quite high and you need a substantial cash injection to get
a new car of similar specification. If you are buying on personal
contract purchase, keeping the car will mean finding the large
final payment.

So, having decided to change cars, you must now decide how.

Clean up

However you decide to part with the car (unless it is scrapped) it must make a good impression. A dealer may have the experience to see through the dirt to assess its true condition but is likely to be more impressed with a clean car, which also gives the impression it has been well cared for. It also means they can give you the best price because they can see what they're getting and it won't need a lot of preparation for sale.

If you sell it privately, it is well worth getting it pristine, even if you pay for a full valet. Private buyers can't always tell what is easily removed surface dirt and what is going to be difficult to put right. Furthermore, they are easily impressed by an exceptionally clean car. Some are so impressed they assume it is as pristine mechanically.

Insight

I am always amazed at the effect a very clean car has when selling it privately. I have sold two cars privately where the buyers were so impressed they looked at little beyond how clean they were: one didn't even want to look under the bonnet. With a wise buyer, cleanliness does little more than create a good first impression, but with these two men it completely sold the car to them on the basis that if it looked clean it was 'clean' in every respect, which is very unwise.

If your car has any minor damage, like small dents and scratches or tears in the seats, you might consider Smart repairs. See Chapter 8 for help on cleaning the car and Smart repairs.

Servicing and testing

If a service or MOT is nearly due, get them done, especially if selling privately. This shows you have confidence in the car and, in the case of the MOT, means you can't be accused of selling an unroadworthy car. If you are selling privately, most buyers expect to get a car with at least six months' MOT still valid and won't want to buy something that needs servicing soon.

Valuation

Before you trade-in or sell your car, you need to know how much it is worth. There are plenty of car price guides available in newsagents that give you an idea, though these can be optimistic especially on trade-in values. The used car valuation bible, Glass's, now offers an online valuation service for a fee (see www.glass.co.uk) though some car sales sites also offer free valuations. It is sensible to get more than one to get a good idea.

However, be honest with yourself. Don't choose a low mileage, good condition valuation if your car isn't. Low mileage is anything below about 10,000 miles a year and good condition doesn't mean 'good if you ignore the scratches'.

Top tip

Print out online valuations so you can use them to back up your valuation arguments, especially when selling privately.

If you sell privately, it also pays to look for similar cars being sold locally to see what others are asking (remember, this isn't what they get). There may be local reasons why a model varies from the national valuation. It might be seen as trendy in one place and common in another. It may have a bad reputation where the marque's dealer is not up to scratch. It may not suit the area: few in the northern isles want convertibles.

You now have an idea of what the car is worth and, therefore, what you can afford to spend on the new car. Now you have to decide how to sell it.

Trade-in vs private sale

Trade-in pros	Trade-in cons
Simple to do	You don't get as much for the car
Sell and buy in one deal	Dealers may not be interested in very old cars
No advertising	May affect discounts on new cars
No buyers messing you around	
An expert handles registration matters	

Private sales pros	Private sales cons
You get more money	More hassle
You only have to haggle one deal when you buy a new car	You have to advertise
Old cars fetch much more money privately	You get messed around by 'buyers'
	You bring strangers to your home
	You must handle registration matters

Trade-in

There is a lot to be said for the simplicity of trading-in. However, if your car is old or unpopular, a trade-in might not be the best deal. Most dealers don't want very old cars on their forecourts unless they are a used-car dealer specializing in older cars and even then they have limits.

The trade-in can work for and against you in getting a good deal. If a dealer wants to offer a good deal he can balance the trade-in price and new car discounts. If the manufacturer says he can't go beyond a certain point on discounting the new car, he can offer you more for the trade-in. He knows how much profit he has to play with on both the new car and selling your old one. However, if he wants to make more from you he can claim to be giving you a great discount on the new car, while taking that money off the trade-in.

PICKING A DEALER

If you are buying a new car it is worth visiting more than one dealer for the marque you intend buying to see who does the best deal.

You are likely to get the best trade-in price from a dealer selling the same marque, but that need not be a problem if you want to change makes. Most dealers are part of a group so if you want to change from a Jeep to a Land Rover, the dealer passes your Jeep on to the group's Jeep dealership. Some groups also have big used-car outlets for trade-ins of all makes.

Private sales

You get the most money selling a car privately. Expect to get somewhere between the trade-in value and what a dealer would sell it for. You can't expect as much as a dealer would get because you can't offer the backup and neither does the buyer have the same legal protection.

WHERE TO ADVERTISE

If it is a very cheap car your best advertising medium is a local newspaper because the rates are low and buyers at this end of the market do not want to travel far. If the car is worth more, the local paper can still offer a cheap way of selling it especially as many newspaper groups now tie in their paper adverts with a web service that covers all the newspapers in their group. This means buyers who are prepared to travel a little further can look at adverts placed in any of the group's newspapers, anywhere in the country.

There are also many regional and national car-selling publications in the UK with some, like *Autotrader*, being a national publication with regional editions. Most of these also tie in with a website. The advantage of doing it this way is that for one fee you get a printed advert for those without internet access and a web advert for those with. In many cases you can place the advert online, which gives you more control over how it looks.

But don't forget the very cheap options of a card in your local newsagents and putting a sign in the car. If you do put a sign in the car either make sure it does not obstruct your view or print it on card so you can prop it in the windscreen when you park.

Top tip

Why not do it as a banner across a windscreen-wide sun blind?

PICTURE THIS

Pictures draw attention to the advert, especially if they are in colour and your car is a bright shade. They also save people asking 'is it the mark one or two' because they can see it. If it is an unusual car it also means people can see it's 'one of those'. But a bad picture can be just as much of a hindrance.

Don't:

▶ *take the picture of a dirty car on your partially shaded drive between the dustbins*
▶ *take a picture where you have to use a wide-angle lens to get it in: this will distort the car's shape in the picture*
▶ *use flash because reflective number plates bounce it straight back at the camera, fooling the exposure.*

Do:

▶ *pick a nice day*
▶ *wash the car (you only have to do one side)*
▶ *drive somewhere where you can get an uncluttered background and have the space to move around the car*
▶ *take cleaning stuff with you because there are bound to be messy roadworks on the way*
▶ *go for a front three-quarter view, photographed from about your waist height*
▶ *if it has good alloy wheels, turn the steering slightly so that the wheel nearest the camera is more visible*
▶ *if you do not have a digital camera on which you can see how it looks, take several pictures at different settings. Very pale or dark cars may fool the exposure*
▶ *almost fill the frame, but leave space around the car in case the publication needs to crop it to a set shape.*

Insight

Have a look at the shape your chosen advertising outlet uses. Most cameras give an oblong shape, so if the advert has a square space you need to leave room on either side of the car for it to be cropped. If it has a longer oblong than your camera's shape, you must leave space above and below the car. Before uploading pictures to websites, check whether they have limits on file sizes or the physical size of the picture. Even the simplest photo editing software allows you to change these things. If there is a file size limit it is better to reduce the pixel size of the picture than to use jpeg compression because the latter can make the picture so fuzzy it may as well not be there.

WRITE STUFF

The wording of your advert is important. Don't waste space by putting in meaningless phrases like 'First to see it will buy': this is not information the buyer needs.

You must accurately give the make, model and version of the car. So, you don't say 'Fiesta 1.4' you say 'Ford Fiesta 1.4i Zetec Climate three-door' because that tells the would-be buyer exactly what it is and if they've done their homework they know it's the 1.4 petrol with the Zetec trim level, air conditioning and heated windscreen.

The advert must also give:

- *price*
- *age*
- *mileage*
- *number of owners*
- *length of MOT*
- *whether it has a full service history (FSH)*
- *colour*
- *fuel type*
- *engine size*
- *gearbox*
- *what equipment it has.*

You might also state its condition, but you must be honest because the advert is proof against you if it proved not to be 'well kept'.

PRICE

The price should be a few hundred above the figure you want. Oddly, people are fooled by knocking the odd £50 off because £9,950 doesn't look as much as £10,000 but do not put 'or near offer' because that suggests you are too willing to drop in price or are not sure of its value. You can shorten the price by saying £10K because most people now know K stands for kilo or 1,000.

AGE

Give the car's age with the year letter or number and the actual year. The UK's year letters cover more than one year, so buyers want to know if an X-reg is 2000 or 2001 or if a 2001 car is X or Y. With numbers, if you say '06' you could mean it is a 2006 model, which could be 06 or 56 registration, while a 56-reg can also be a 2007 model.

These differences add or subtract a few hundred from the value and can mean changes in specification.

MILEAGE

Give mileage to the nearest 1,000. As with price you can use K to shorten it.

OWNERS

State how many owners it has had as shown on the registration document, though if you're the first owner say 'owned from new' to avoid people thinking 'one owner' means one plus you.

SERVICE HISTORY

If you have kept a full record put 'FSH' (Full Service History) but if it has always been serviced by the franchised dealer, say 'Dealer FSH'. If you do not have the full history, perhaps because a previous owner didn't keep one, put SH (Service History) or 'partial SH' and explain to people who call.

COLOUR

Stating colour seems odd if the advert has a colour picture, but some people don't realize the car pictured is the actual car and some colours don't reproduce well, with metallics often looking non-metallic.

FUEL AND GEARBOX

Give the fuel type because some people don't realize 1.4TDi means it is a diesel and 1.4i means it is petrol injection. Also say if the car is turbo-charged and, if your car is available with engines of the same size but different power, state which power it is. Don't just say manual or automatic gearbox but say how many speeds it has.

EQUIPMENT

You can't list all the equipment a car has but make sure you list any extras fitted. With standard equipment, go for the highlights people seek out like sunroofs, power steering, air conditioning, safety equipment, leather seats, electric windows and mirrors, remote central locking and anything unusual.

INITIAL RESISTANCE

Used-car adverts often use abbreviations to keep within the word count but think carefully before using them. Most people understand FSH, **PAS** for power assisted steering and **ABS** for anti-lock brakes but will everyone make the connection between RCL and remote central locking or ESR for electric sunroof? Your car's specification may include new technology with acronyms commonly used in the motor industry, like **ESP** (electronic stability programme) but not everyone knows what they mean.

Also look at how the advertising medium sees hyphenated words. 'Five-speed' could be seen as one or two words but '5sp' should be one.

DETAILS

If you are advertising in a national or regional medium it is sensible to put the name of the town you live in so buyers can see how far away you are, though websites usually allow buyers to state a distance in searches. Don't give just a mobile phone number because that is a trick used by dishonest traders (see Chapter 3). Give a landline number and a mobile if you are not at home during the day. Most people, though, would realize that if they didn't get an answer during the day, they should try in the evening.

Finally, add NC for 'no canvassers' or you will get other advertising media pestering you to advertise with them.

Keep a copy of the advert near the phone so you know what is in it when you speak to prospective buyers.

Dealing with buyers

Sadly, you will get time wasters and after a while you can tell who they are because of their lack of knowledge of the car they claim to be interested in buying. Ask people who arrange to come and see the car to call you if they decide not to come and get their phone number, saying this is so you can call if someone else buys it or if you can't make the appointment. If your home is difficult to find, have some directions you can email, fax or dictate.

FIRST CONTACT

Answer callers' questions truthfully and if you don't know the answer, say so. Don't say things that bring the person to you on false pretences because nobody is likely to buy the car if they feel you can't be trusted.

If someone asks if you will move on the price you tell them to come and look at it and see if they think it is worth less than you have asked. Of course, you would be prepared to take less to sell it, but you don't want to sound too eager.

If your insurance does not give full cover to other drivers, make that clear to callers and say that if they want to drive it they will have to bring proof of full cover. If you allow someone to drive uninsured, you are also committing an offence and if they have an accident when driving with only third-party cover, you could have trouble getting the cost of repairs or replacement from them.

Fix a time for them to come. If you agree on 'Saturday morning' you have to spend the entire morning waiting for them, but if you fix '10 a.m. Saturday' you know to ring them if they are not there by 10.30 a.m.

SAFE NOT SORRY

Don't feel bad about treating a potential buyer with caution. You do not know them and they should understand that, for this reason, you can't leave them alone with the car keys, let them take a test drive alone or expect a woman owner to drive off alone with a strange man. If they make a fuss, make it clear you are not prepared to do business with them.

> ## Insight
>
> Sadly, people will tell you this is the car of their dreams and sound very enthusiastic, then not turn up and not bother to call to say they are not coming. The last time I sold a car, one person stressed he was prepared to make an 80-mile trip to see it because he was so keen on owning a Land Rover Defender – 'always wanted one, boyhood dream, etc, etc …' When he didn't turn up I called and got his wife who said they had set out, discussed it as they drove and that he had changed his mind so instead they were going shopping. At least by getting his number I had saved myself wasting a morning waiting for him and could phone someone else who had left details and who bought it that afternoon.

SELLING AND HAGGLING

Show them over the car, highlighting the plus points. Don't lie about faults but then again, don't point out the scratches. Show them any documentation, but don't let them take it out of your sight and don't leave them alone with it.

When it comes to haggling have an absolute minimum price and stick to it. If you got it wrong, you might regret sticking to it in a week or two if you haven't sold the car, but you'll also kick yourself if you accept less than you expected from the first caller.

Make them make an offer: many people will ask you how much you want, to which the answer is 'as much as I can get'. If you advertised it at £9,950 and will accept £9,500, you lose out if you say that and the buyer was thinking of offering £9,800. If it is obvious they won't make an offer, just knock £50 off the asking price to get things moving.

Be polite but firm and don't feel insulted if someone offers a lot less than you asked. Keep a note of phone numbers so that if the car doesn't sell you can always call those you couldn't agree a price with to see if they are still interested, but if your price was right it shouldn't come to that.

Payment

If someone says they want to buy the car but wants a vehicle inspection or needs to come back later with the money, it is reasonable for you to ask for a deposit. Write a dated receipt saying who it is paid from and to, what the agreed price is and what car it relates to. Also state that the deposit will only be returned if the vehicle fails an inspection.

With cash you only need to be sure the notes are genuine. A cheque for the value of a car is only really safe if you wait for it to clear. A bankers' draft is the safest form of payment, but forged ones do spring up from time to time so it is best to only accept one during hours when you can call the issuing bank. Unfortunately, bank hours don't usually coincide with the times of day that people can come and collect cars and there is no way round that. This is why it is important to get as much proof as possible of who you are selling the car to.

Give them a dated, written receipt stating how much was paid and giving the full details of the car and the addresses of those involved and either photocopy it or make two receipts. These days it pays to put a time of exchange on the receipt because you are liable for traffic offences committed in the car until the DVLA have been informed of the change of ownership. With a timed receipt you have some evidence that you were not driving the car at the time.

Paperwork

All developed countries register cars, therefore they also have
change of ownership regulations. In the UK you must, by law,
inform the DVLA that you have sold the car and the registration
form has notes explaining which colour-coded and numbered
sections must be filled in. There are separate sections to be filled in
if you sell it to a dealer and if you sell it privately. If you trade it in,
the dealer will guide you through the process. If you sell privately,
you have to make sure you do it properly.

In a private sale, there are three sections to be filled in. On the
main body of the form you need the buyer's name, address and
driving licence number in the green section and then you both sign
a red declaration at the bottom of the page. You send this page
to the DVLA. On the opposite page, below the section filled in if
you trade the car in to a dealer, is a green 'New Keeper Supplement'
which is also filled in with the buyer's name and address and which
the buyer keeps until the new registration document arrives.
(See Chapter 3.)

Top tip

> Do not part with any of this documentation until you are
> sure you have full payment.

Auctions

Car dealers and fleets often use auctions to get rid of cars they
don't want but for the private individual it is not usually a viable
proposition unless it is a collectable car. You are likely to get the
least for the car selling it this way and must be sure you understand
what fees you pay on the sale. However, at least you do not have
the hassle of advertising it and having to deal with phone calls and
buyers. For a seller, online auctions are more like placing an advert.

Scrapping it

A car gets to the end of its useful life because repairs needed
to keep it legal cost more than it is worth. Do not be tempted
to dump it. Apart from the environmental and safety concerns,
it is illegal and even if you remove the number plates there are
still ways of tracing the owner.

Car makers have been ensuring the recyclability of their products
for years and some have been marking all the plastics in their cars
with recycling information since the 1980s. So if your car has to be
scrapped, try to ensure it is fully recycled by taking it to a properly
equipped scrapyard.

Under the EU End of Life Directive, car makers in Europe have set
up arrangements to ensure their cars are recycled when scrapped,
and this came into operation in the UK on 1 January 2007.
Manufacturers who have sold cars in the UK have contracted
with either Autogreen or Cartakeback to provide 'End of Life'
facilities who issue owners with a DVLA Certificate of Destruction
to allow the car to be deregistered. To find your marque's nearest
'Authorized Treatment Facility', www.cartakeback.com has
an online search facility or can be called on 0845 2573233, or
Autogreen can tell you your nearest ATF on 0800 5422002, their
website is www.autogreen.org (no online search was available
when we visited). Collection can be arranged and is free if you are
more than 30 miles from your manufacturer's nearest facility.

Sadly, you are unlikely to get anything for your wreck because
the value of recycled materials is generally less than the cost of
recovering them.

Top tip

If the car does not have a valid MOT, you can't drive it to
the scrap yard.

10 THINGS TO REMEMBER

1 *However you sell your car, clean it first.*

2 *Use printed and online price guides to get an idea of its value.*

3 *Trade-in is easiest but a private sale gets you more money.*

4 *Trade-in might not be viable with a very old or undesirable car.*

5 *It is worth taking time to get a decent picture of the car
   for adverts.*

6 *Do not waste your advert's word limit with useless phrases –
   give useful facts only.*

7 *Do not lie in your advert.*

8 *When people call in response to adverts, answer their
   questions honestly, fix a visiting time and get a phone number
   for anyone who says they are coming.*

9 *Do not allow people to take test drives alone or without proof
   of insurance.*

10 *Do not part with ownership documents until you have been
   fully paid.*

Taking it further

BREAKDOWN ORGANIZATIONS

The phone numbers given below are for membership inquiries. The websites contain a lot of helpful motoring information and links to their car checking services.

Automobile Association (AA) www.theaa.co.uk 0800 0852721.
Britannia Rescue www.britanniarescue.com 0800 591563.
Green Flag www.greenflag.co.uk 0845 2461557.
Royal Automobile Club (RAC) www.rac.co.uk 0800 0960732.

GOVERNMENT BODIES

Insight

> I'll apologize in advance if any of the web addresses or phone numbers below are out of date. Unfortunately, Government agencies seem to change these more frequently than most organizations, making it difficult to keep up with them.

The various Government motoring agencies are all represented on the Directgov website at www.direct.gov.uk where you can download forms, get information and tax your car online.

Driver and Vehicle Licensing Agency (DVLA), responsible for all licensing and registration matters, www.dft.gov.uk/dvla. Driver inquiries 0300 7906801. Vehicle inquiries 0300 7906802.

Vehicle Operator Services Agency (VOSA), responsible for MOTs and construction and use matters (MOT checks, see opposite), www.dft.gov.uk/vosa. The local office is in the phone book. Headquarters: 0300 1239000.

Department for Transport's 'Think!' road safety campaign for general road safety information offering downloadable pamphlets including one on child safety seats: www.dft.gov.uk/think.

TRADE ASSOCIATIONS

Society of Motor Manufacturers and Traders (SMMT), UK motor industry body, www.smmt.co.uk. Consumer advice line 0800 6920825.

Retail Motor Industry Federation (RMIF), trade body for dealers and garages in England and Wales, www.rmif.co.uk, consumer advice line as SMMT.

Scottish Motor Trade Association (SMTA), Scottish equivalent of the RMIF, www.smta.co.uk, 0131 331 5510.

Association of British Insurers (ABI), trade body for UK insurers with lots of insurance information on the website, www.abi.org.uk, 020 7600 3333.

TRADING STANDARDS

Your local office is in the phone book but may be listed under your county or metropolitan council. The national Trading Standards website, at www.tradingstandards.gov.uk, has a great deal of advice on car buying and garage services as well as small claims court information and a search facility to find your local Trading Standards office.

USED CAR CHECKS

AA Car Data Check, used-car status check, www.aacardatacheck.com.

Glass's, online used-car valuation service, www.glass.co.uk (the site has other useful car buying information and links to the AA Car Data Check).

HPI Equifax, used-car status check, www.hpicheck.com, 0845 3008905.

RAC car examinations and used-car status check, www.rac.co.uk, 0800 9755867.

VOSA MOT Certificate validation, www.motinfo.gov.uk, 0870 3300444.

SCRAPPING CARS IN THE UK

Check which company your car maker is contracted to.

www.autogreen.org, 0800 5422002.
www.cartakeback.com, 0845 2573233.

OTHER INFORMATION

All motor manufacturers and importers have websites giving details of their cars and their dealer locations and most have a search facility for their dealers' used-car stock. There are also hundreds of sites advertising used cars for sale and most car magazines have sites with useful information and, in many cases, at least shortened versions of their road tests.

Glossary

4×4, 4WD Abbreviations for four-wheel drive (the former is a military one meaning four wheels, four driven)

ABS Anti-brake-lock system. Electronics that stop the brakes locking to prevent a skid

Airbag A safety device inflated by gas from a pyrotechnic cartridge to cushion occupants against impacts

Air con Air conditioning

Alternator The car's generator

Anti-freeze A coolant additive that prevents freezing, raises its boiling point and prevents corrosion

Bar A metric measurement of air pressure (1 bar = 14.5 psi)

Bead The reinforced band that holds a tyre onto the wheel

bhp Brake horsepower, the usual measurement of engine power in the UK and America

Biodiesel Diesel made from plant sources. Most diesel is a mix of bio and fossil fuel

Bioethanol A fuel from plant sources that can be used with some engines which run on any mix of petrol and bioethanol

Biofuels Fuels from renewable plant sources

Blow-out When a tyre suddenly, and sometimes explosively, deflates

Bluetooth Wireless connection between mobile phones and other portable data technology. Can provide hands-free mobile phone connection in a car but functionality varies

Business manager A title often used for the person in a motor dealership who specializes in customer finance

Camshaft A shaft with eccentrically shaped lobes that open and close the valves which let the fuel/air mixture into the engine and the exhaust gasses out

Cambelt A drive belt that drives the camshafts from the crankshaft. Also called a timing belt

Carburettor A device for mixing the fuel with the right amount of air to supply the engine. Now replaced by much more efficient electronic fuel injection

Catalytic converter A device in the exhaust which uses catalysts to clean the emissions by changing poisonous gases to less harmful ones. Also called a cat or catalyst

Cetane number The measurement of diesel fuel quality. Distributors put out different cetane ratings for summer and winter

Climate control Automatic air conditioning

Clutch A friction-plate system that disengages a manual gearbox from the engine

CO_2 Carbon dioxide, a greenhouse gas emitted as a result of combustion

Combustion chamber The area of the engine's cylinder in which fuel and air are burnt

Continuously variable transmission (CVT) An automatic gearbox with no fixed ratios. It uses belts and pulleys to maintain optimum 'ratios' for the demands on the engine

Cylinders The holes in the engine in which the pistons move up and down. They may be arranged inline, in a V or horizontally opposed

Differential A system of gears that allows driven wheels to rotate at different speeds when cornering. All cars have at least one, but full-time 4WD requires one in each axle and one in the middle

DIN The German standards institute

Dipstick A stick for measuring how much fluid something contains. All cars have an engine oil dipstick but they may also have them for transmission oil and power steering fluid

Disc brake A brake where the friction pads grip a disc attached to the wheel hub

Distributor The part of the ignition that distributes the power to each sparkplug in turn. Now replaced by electronics

Drum brake A brake where curved friction 'shoes' press out against the inside of a drum to which the wheel is attached

DVLA The Driver and Vehicle Licensing Agency. The UK government body responsible for driving licences and vehicle registration

Engine management The electronics that run the engine's ignition and fuel-injection

EPAS Electronic power-assisted steering

ESP Electronic stability programme. A device that stops the car drifting sideways if you corner too fast

Euro1 to 6 European exhaust emission standards begun in 1992. Euro5 came in 2009 and Euro6 is due in 2014

Flexifuel A Ford term for cars run on bioethanol and petrol

FSH Full service history (seen in used-car adverts)

Fuel cells The power source for future cars. The cell generates electricity by combining hydrogen fuel with oxygen in the air. Water is the only emission

Gasket A membrane of soft, flexible material that seals the join between two metal components

Gearbox A system of gears that enables the car's engine speed to be matched to the road speed to optimize the use of power and torque

g/Km Carbon dioxide (and other exhaust gas) output is measured in grammes emitted per kilometre. The UK's road and company car taxes are based on this

Glowplug A device that warms the combustion chambers in a diesel to aid starting

Hatchback A car which has a rear door instead of a boot. Originally they were small but now they come in all sizes

Hazard warning lights A switch that brings on all four indicators at once. Compulsory in Europe and some other markets

Head restraints Cushions that rise above the seat back to stop the head whipping back in an accident and causing 'whiplash' neck injuries

HOAT Hybrid organic acid technology. The latest anti-freeze technology used by several car manufacturers (see Chapter 5)

Horsepower The usual measurement of engine power in the UK and America

HP Hire purchase when referring to credit, or metric horsepower (hp) when applied to engines (an alternative abbreviation to the German PS)

HPI Check A vehicle history check. This name comes from the best known company for carrying them out

Hybrid A car powered by a hybrid system which combines a conventional petrol or diesel with an electric motor to reduce emissions

IAT Inorganic acid technology. The original anti-freeze technology (see Chapter 5)

Inertia-reel seatbelt A belt which rolls back into a reel which is locked by sudden movement

Insurance excess The amount of money the insured has to pay on any claim

Isofix A near foolproof system for attaching child seats to cars named after the International Standards Organization

Jacking points Reinforced parts of the car which must be used when jacking it up

Kevlar A fibre by Dupont that is five times stronger than steel. It is used for reinforcing tyres and composite car bodies as well as in bulletproof vests

Kilowatts (Kw) A metric measurement of engine power (1 Kw = 1.341 bhp)

kph Kilometres per hour (1 kph = 0.621 mph)

lb ft Pounds-feet, the usual UK and American way of measuring torque

LED Light emitting diodes – used in instrument lighting, most high level brake lights and some ordinary brake and side lights. Unlike bulbs, they have no filament to burn out so should last the life of the car

Metallic and micatallic paint Paints which have flecks of metal or mica to reflect the light

MOT Originally the Ministry of Transport test, the UK's vehicle roadworthiness test

mpg Miles per gallon. The imperial measurement of fuel consumption

mph Miles per hour

MPV Multi-purpose vehicle. A car with a one-box body that seats up to seven and has versatile load-carrying ability. Also called a people-carrier and known in the USA as a 'van'. (Examples include the Renault Espace and the Chrysler Voyager.)

NCAP New Car Assessment Programme. Independent crash safety testing programmes. There are European and American NCAPs

Newton Metres (Nm) A metric measurement of torque (1 Nm = 5.163 lb ft)

OAT Organic acid technology. An anti-freeze technology (see Chapter 5)

Octane number The measurement of petrol quality (UK standard unleaded is 95 octane)

Particulates Fine particles of soot in the exhaust, usually associated with diesels. Modern diesels with particulate filters emit virtually none

PAS Power assisted steering

PCP Personal contract purchase. A form of car-buying credit with low monthly payments (see Chapter 2)

PDI Pre-delivery inspection

Pearlescant paint Paint with a pearl-like sheen

Pounds-feet How you say 'lb ft', the measurement of torque

PS Metric measurement of power from the German 'Pferdestärken', meaning horsepower (1 PS = 0.986 bhp)

Revs Short form for revolutions per minute (rpm) denoting engine speed

RMIF Retail Motor Industry Federation. Motor dealers' and garages' body in England and Wales

rpm Revolutions per minute. The speed something rotates at, especially engines

Sale of Goods Act The law that gives those buying from a dealer protection against mis-sold goods

Satellite Navigation or sat nav A system that combines digital mapping with signals from geo-positioning satellites to provide directions

SAE Society of Automotive Engineers. They set standards for many things in cars

Seatbelt pre-tensioners Devices which take the slack out of the belt in a crash

Sequential shift A facility on automatic gearboxes allowing manual changes by tapping either the gear lever or steering wheel-controls

Side repeater indicator A little indicator on the front wing or door mirror

Smart repairs Localized repairs to minor damage avoiding replacement (see Chapters 8 and 11)

SMMT Society of Motor Manufacturers and Traders. The industry trade body in the UK

Sparkplug The device which ignites the fuel/mixture in a petrol car (sometimes called a sparking plug)

SMTA Scottish Motor Trade Association. Motor dealers' and garages' body in Scotland

Surfactants Substances which get between dirt and a surface, used in many car care products

SUV Sports utility vehicle. An American abbreviation now widely adopted to differentiate passenger 4×4s, like the Range Rover, from working ones (utilities), like the Land Rover Defender

Timing belt Another name for the cambelt

Tiptronic The first sequential shift (see above) developed by Porsche

Torque Twisting power. In cars it is often called pulling power and gives an engine driving flexibility

Torque converter An oil-filled device that takes the place of a clutch in an automatic transmission

Transmission Everything that transmits the drive from the engine to the wheels, including the clutch, gearbox, drive shafts and differentials

Transponder A device that sends and responds to a signal. Cars use them for remote central locking, immobilizer systems and tracking devices

Vehicle Identification Check (VIC) A notification by the DVLA to flag up cars that have been seriously damaged and written off (see 'Write-offs' in Chapter 3)

VOSA Vehicle Operator Services Agency. Formerly the Vehicle Inspectorate. The UK body responsible for enforcing vehicle construction and use laws and for roadworthiness testing

Wheelbase The measurement between the front and rear wheels. A longer wheel base generally means more interior space

Wheel brace A long handled spanner for undoing wheel nuts. Called a 'tire iron' in America

Whiplash Potentially serious injuries to the neck caused by the head being whipped backwards. See head restraint

Index